CITY OF TRURO
A LOCOMOTIVE LEGEND

EDITED BY

NIGEL HARRIS

Silver Link Publishing

5 HAWK ST, CARNFORTH, LANCASHIRE, LA5 9LA

C000048041

City of Truro: a locomotive legend.
   1. City of Truro (Locomotive)
   I. Harris, Nigel
   625.2'61'9042   TJ603.4.G/2G73

ISBN 0-947971-02-5

Copyright © Silver Link Publishing. 1985.

First published in the United Kingdom. July 1985.

ISBN 0 947971 02 5

All rights reserved. No part of this publication may be reproduced, stored in a retrieval system, transmitted in any form by any means electronic or mechanical, or photocopied, or recorded by any other information storage and retrieval system without prior permission in writing from the publisher.

Designed by Nigel Harris.
Front cover design by Phil Cousins.

Typeset by Pen to Print, Colne, Lancashire.
Printed by Netherwood Dalton & Co. Ltd., Huddersfield, Yorkshire.

CONTENTS

Acknowledgements

MANY people have played a part in the production of this book, but the publisher would particularly like to thank the National Railway Museum and the Severn Valley Railway for their detailed assistance. At the NRM, Keeper Dr J.A. Coiley, Assistant Keeper Peter Semmens and Chief Mechanical Engineer John Bellwood made time in their schedules to contribute to this book while the library staff, especially John Edgington and Phil Atkins helped considerably with picture research and historical detail. On the SVR thanks are due to Public Relations Officer Neil Howard, General Manager Michael Draper and Chief Engineer Alun Rees. Credit is also due to Keith Beck and Dick Riley for their expertise and enthusiastic assistance.

Finally, many thanks indeed to photographers too numerous to mention individually, who have provided such marvellous illustrations.

Front cover: In low evening sunshine, No. 3440 *City of Truro* accelerates away from Swindon with the 5.32 pm passenger to Bristol, via Badminton, in the summer of 1960. *Dr J.A. Coiley.*

Back cover: No. 3440 *City of Truro* stands on the middle road at Bath Spa station shortly after overhaul whilst working the 10.5 am Bristol Temple Meads – Swindon local of March 25 1957. This was a regular Swindon works running in turn. *Ivo Peters.*

Previous page: *City of Truro* makes haste on Hatton Bank on June 16 1957, en route from Swindon to Birmingham Snow Hill, with the return run of a SLS special. *Tom Williams/Patrick Russell Collection.*

Opposite page: The exciting combination of GWR 4-4-0 No. 3440 *City of Truro* and MR 'Compound' 4-4-0 No. 1000 make a spirited departure from Doncaster as part of an Ian Allan Locospotters special from Kings Cross to Doncaster, April 20 1960. *Eric Oldham.*

FOREWORD
Dr J.A. Coiley MA PhD
Keeper, National Railway Museum

City of Truro. To railway enthusiasts and I suspect many others, this name evokes nostalgic memories of the golden days of railways and steam locomotives in particular. The performance of *City of Truro* in 1904 was the stuff legends are made of — 100 mph by train recorded for the first time. In retrospect however it is probably the remarkable competitive business initiative the railways displayed at the time which today we should consider more impressive.

Whatever the circumstances, *City of Truro* belongs to the heroic age of railway history. For this reason I am grateful for the opportunity to say how pleased the National Railway Museum is to have been able to agree to the restoration of *City of Truro* to main-line working order again, as part of our contribution to the Great Western 150 anniversary celebrations. This would not have been possible, however, without the support and co-operation of many enthusiasts and the staff of several organisations including the Science Museum, the Great Western Museum of the Borough of Thamesdown, the Severn Valley Railway, the Steam Locomotive Operators' Association, British Rail Engineering Limited, Swindon and British Rail, Western Region.

I hope this book will help those interested in our railway history and especially that of the Great Western railway, to appreciate the legend of the *City of Truro* more fully. Furthermore, I hope it will encourage them to go to see *City of Truro* in action and, if possible, to ride behind this famous locomotive while they can, even if not at 100 mph!

J.A. COILEY

J.A. COILEY

GWR 4-4-0 No. 3440 City of Truro **skirts the rock face at Nottingham Victoria station, en route to Scotland, for excursion duties, on August 26 1959. This station closed on September 4 1967.** *T.G. Hepburn/Rail Archive Stephenson.*

CHAPTER 1:

THE GWR 'CITIES': THEIR PLACE IN LOCOMOTIVE HISTORY

John Bellwood
C Eng MI Mech E MCIT MBIM

Chief Mechanical Engineer, National Railway Museum

A photograph which is not all it appears to be. The numberplate and part of the nameplate have been superimposed onto a works view of No. 3434 *City of Birmingham* to give an impression of No. 3440 *City of Truro* in original condition. It was in this form that the locomotive is reputed to have reached 102.3 mph in May 1904. *BR/OPC.*

IN THE simplest, briefest terms, it can be said the objective of the National Railway Museum at York is: "to tell the continuing story of railways in Britain and the British influence on railways overseas". There is, of course, far more to it than that. Apart from the conservation and interpretation of the actual objects in the Collection, the spread of railways has had a significant effect on the social, economic and political development of most nations over the past 160 years or so.

It is however the steam locomotive which has attracted the most attention, with the Rainhill trials of 1829 probably first awakening widespread public interest in the subject. Perhaps one day someone will produce a reasonably accurate assessment of just how many steam locomotives have actually worked in Britain and how many more were built here for service abroad. On the basis that the newly Nationalised British Railways inherited some 20,000 locomotives from the 'big four' companies on January 1 1948, and it has been estimated that something like the same number were then in industrial use, the final figure must be an enormous one. In this context, it can be argued that any locomotive which justifies a place in the National Collection of just under 100 examples must be something special.

Right: GWR 4-4-0 No. 3395 *Aden*, of the 'Atbara' class, from which the 'City' or '3700' class was developed. Note the parallel boiler. *R.S. Carpenter Collection.*

Below right: 'Atbara' 4-4-0 No. 3405 *Mauritius* was rebuilt with a Churchward Standard No. 4 boiler in September 1902 as the prototype 'City'. The tapered boiler and distinctive Belpaire firebox are clearly evident. Note also the plain, tapered cast-iron chimney. *R.C. Riley Collection.*

There are of course some very significant omissions. It has to be remembered, however, that this country, which gave railways to the world, was one of the last to set up a National Museum devoted to the subject. Serious collecting on a national scale did not start until the 1950s, by which time much had been lost forever. Inevitably, some less-important items found their way into the Collection just because they had survived until then. There are also many different criteria which can be applied when attempting to decide what is, or will in future be, considered as being of particular significance in the development of railways. Not all the locomotives in the Collection can be said to be included on the basis of technical excellence, or innovation which had a major effect on future development. One can think of at least one example where the livery and outline seems to be the main reason for inclusion!

So where does *City of Truro* fit in and just how significant was the class in general and this locomotive in particular? The '3700' or 'City' Class of GWR 4-4-0 tender engines were something of a hybrid, introduced in September 1902 when the 'Atbara' class locomotive No. 3405 *Mauritius*, then only one-year old, was rebuilt with a Churchward Standard No. 4 boiler. It is interesting to speculate whether the reason for the rebuilding was that the 'Atbara's' were considered to be underboilered, or was it just a convenient way of providing a test-bed for the new design of boiler? Ten new engines, including No. 3440 *City of Truro*, were built in 1903 and the class was further increased in numbers by the rebuilding of another nine 'Atbara's' in the years 1907–9. During the period 1903–13 a total of 17 'Badminton' 4-4-0s also carried the Standard No. 4 boiler and so may be regarded as 'temporary Cities'.

Although doubts have been cast on the accuracy of the claimed 102.3 mph maximum achieved by *City of Truro* whilst descending Wellington Bank on May 9 1904, there is no doubt the Dean type passenger locomotives could, and did, attain some very high speeds by the standards of the day. Mechanically, apart from driving wheel diameter, the various four-coupled locomotives of the GWR then followed the same general pattern of double frames and 18in. × 26in. cylinders with slide valves positioned underneath, having a maximum travel of 4⅝in. Boilers, however, varied considerably.

Considering the ten 'Cities' built new in 1903, it could be argued that they were of a somewhat outdated express passenger design, compared with contemporary practice on other main-line companies. Certainly double frames were generally considered obsolete, although the GWR was to give the form a new lease of life with the 'Earls' built 1936–9. The frames for these were, however, 'recovered' from withdrawn 'Bulldogs' — perhaps an economy measure to partially offset the relatively high building costs of the typical GWR locomotive of the day! It is not clear why the GWR continued double-framed construction long after it had been given up elsewhere. An exten-

sive frame strengthening programme became necessary to keep the locomotives so-fitted in service and, compared with the single-plate frame, double frames were heavier and cost more to construct. There was also a greater liability for the crank-axle to fracture, although on the positive side they made it possible to increase bearing surfaces considerably, thus reducing the risk of overheating.

In other respects a relatively small, inside-cylindered 4-4-0 with a tractive effort of 17,790 lbs could not really be considered as front-line express passenger motive power, in 1903. Although the 'Cities' were of similar size to the GER 'Claude Hamilton' class introduced in 1900, they could hardly be compared with the GNR large-boilered 'Atlantic' of 1902 or NER Class 'S' 4-6-0 of 1899.

At a time when train loads were increasing with the demand for better passenger facilities in the form of corridor bogie-stock and dining facilities, the potential for increased haulage capacity was an important factor. The greatest single step forward yet to be made was the application of superheating. This cannot be said to have revolutionised the performance of the 'Cities' when

Some contemporary locomotives . . .

Above: Webb four-cylinder compound 4-4-0 No. 1941 *Alfred the Great*, built by the LNWR at Crewe in 1901. This was an unsuccessful design, modified by Whale and subsequently rebuilt as a simple engine.

Right: NER 'S' class 4-6-0 No. 2001 (built 1899) was Britain's first express passenger 4-6-0. This is a works photograph of No. 2005. Only four of the 40 built were superheated and whilst not an outstanding success they pointed the way forward for a popular type — especially on the GWR.

Below right: Ivatt large-boiler Atlantic introduced in 1902 on the Great Northern Railway. When later fitted with 32-element superheaters after 30 years at work, this design proved capable of still mastering all but the heaviest trains, and were capable of deputising for the 'Pacifics'. The pioneer No. 251 has an honoured place in the National Collection.

Below: GER 'Claude Hamilton' 4-4-0 No. 1900 *Claud Hamilton*, introduced in 1900. Although shown here in early LNER livery, No. 1900 appears as built, with 4ft 5in diameter boiler and round-top firebox.

All: National Railway Museum

fitted later in their working life, whereas the high-superheat GNR 'Atlantics' were still hauling the most prestigious expresses on the East Coast Main Line in the 1930's. The 4-6-0 was destined to be a significant express passenger type until the end of steam traction in Britain, particularly on the GWR. In fact the first of a long line of the Swindon express passenger type emerged on the scene a year earlier than *City of Truro*. Incidentally the last NER 'S' class 4-6-0 of 1899 was still extant in 1951, and it would seem unfortunate that an example of this class, Britain's first express passenger 4-6-0 type, did not survive into preservation.

Even in the field of contemporary 4-4-0s the 'Cities' cannot be considered as class leaders. Probably one of the best 'turn of the century'

inside cylinder 4-4-0s was the NER class 'R' introduced in 1899. Here was a design which could be said to outclass the 'Cities' in almost every respect. With single frames, a 200 psi working pressure boiler, and piston valves, they proved capable of working the 320-ton 'Flying Scotsman' trains of the day at speeds of up to 70 mph with exceptional reliability. The pioneer member of the class ran 284,000 miles in just over three years before requiring its first general overhaul. Not many steam locomotives of any era achieved that sort of utilisation! Subsequently superheated, the 'R's had a working life extending over 57 years, compared with the 28 year span of the 'Cities'.

The other main development of the period was compounding applied to multi-cylindered locomo-

tives. The GWR imported three De-Glehn type 'Atlantics' from France in 1903–5, which influenced Swindon practice in some design features but not in compounding. The Webb four-cylinder compound express 'Alfred the Great' class 4-4-0, built by the LNWR in 1901–3, did not live up to the class name and was soon altered by Whale. On the other hand, the application of the Smith system to five Johnson three-cylinder 4-4-0's on the Midland Ralway in 1901–3 resulted in the most successful application of compounding in this country. An 'easier to drive' version introduced in 1905 produced, when subsequently superheated, an exceptionally economical locomotive which became the standard express passenger type on the LMS after the Grouping.

To return to the earlier question, it can be seen that in many respects the essential features of the 'City' class were obsolete by the time *Mauritius* received its No. 4 standard boiler, certainly as far as the top-rank express passenger needs of a major trunk route were concerned. The boiler was the one innovative feature which was to influence future GWR practice. The ability to attain a very high speed with a relatively light train is more a factor of mechanical design than steam producing capacity. Ride quality, and in particular a good front-end, are essential features which must have been there in full measure in the Dean express designs. The 100 mph claim may have been disputed but there is no doubt that the 'Cities' were real 'fliers' in their day; second-to-none in this respect. It is however unlikely that a representative of the class would have been preserved had not Rous-Marten been travelling with his stopwatch on the up mail special of May 9 1904. Certainly the GWR did not have the best of reputations throughout its history for the preservation of important examples of its heritage.

Left: The smokebox fittings of No. 3440 *City of Truro*, as painted white during museum display. The plates hinged to the frame around the base of the exhaust 'petticoat', and secured to the blastpipe cap by two substantial clamps, were char deflectors designed to minimise spark emission. Note that the inside of the smokebox door is fitted with a flat plate to protect the dished main door, which was a comparatively expensive item to produce. The protector plate was much cheaper to fit and could be replaced periodically. The smaller crescent shaped plate prevented char accumulating in the door-joint. *National Railway Museum.*

For whatever reason, we are fortunate that an interesting example of late 19th century if not fully representative of early 20th century, express passenger locomotive design is still with us. That such an example was selected for restoration to main line working order in the GWR 150 anniversary year of 1985 is an added bonus. Perhaps this type of operation could be the future role for some of the less technically important examples in the National Collection, when conservation need not be of such primary consideration.

Above right: Midland Railway 4-4-0 No. 2633, a 1901 three-cylinder design using the Smith compound system. Subsequently rebuilt and modified for easier driving, these locomotives were outstandingly economical and were built in large numbers for the LMS after the 1923 Grouping — 195 were built between 1923 and 1932. The pioneer No. 1000 (original number 2631) in superheated form is one of the unique working locomotives in the National Collection.

Right: North Eastern Railway 'R' class 4-4-0 No. 592 — fitted with superheaters in 1915 — with a stopping passenger train at Craigentinny, in the mid-1920s. This class was introduced in 1899.
Both: National Railway Museum.

Left: No. 3433 *City of Bath*, pictured in original condition and coupled to a Dean tender, probably at Westbourne Park shed, which served Paddington until 1906, when Old Oak Common took over this role. Of interest is the jack carried on the locomotive's running plate above the trailing bogie wheel. These were standard GWR locomotive equipment until circa 1906, and were carried in the event of derailments. The locomotive is fitted with square pegs for the headlamps, rather than brackets and is in very clean condition: all brass trim on the bogie and driving wheel splashers is highly polished.

Below left: No. 3716 *City of London* in final rebuilt form, with superheating, top-feed, bigger sandboxes, copper-capped chimney and main-frame strengthening plates. This locomotive was withdrawn in April 1929.
Lens of Sutton.

CHAPTER 2:

MAY 9 1904: A LEGEND IS CREATED

P.W.B. Semmens
MA CChem FRSC MBCS MCIT
Assistant Keeper, National Railway Museum

IN THE West of England, May 9 1904 dawned bright and clear, the perfect visibility enabling the verdant greens of the Devonshire countryside to be enjoyed to the full. At 8 o'clock that morning the Norddeutscher Lloyd liner *Kronprinz Wilhelm* dropped anchor in Plymouth Sound with a load of mail that was more than usually important. Although the first Trans-Atlantic cable had been laid many years earlier by Brunel's *Great Eastern*, the telegraphic system could in no way handle such important transactions as the gold bullion payment for the Panama Canal that was being made on this occasion by the United States to France. In any case, these ocean 'greyhounds', dashing across the Atlantic between Europe and North America, carried much important business and personal mail as well as their complement of passengers, who enjoyed to the full the luxury provided on board during their six-day crossing.

These liners were supreme at sea from the speed point of view, and rapid technological improvements meant there was great rivalry between the different companies and nations operating the famous liners to give the fastest service. To complement the record ocean transits that resulted, the services of the railways were enlisted to speed passengers and mail between the ports and London, then the predominant mercantile centre of the world. Liners bound for Liverpool were later to find it worthwhile to call at Fishguard or Holyhead to transfer their most prestigious loads to rail, giving a significant overall saving in time. For eastbound liners whose ultimate destination was North Germany, there was a great incentive to call at Plymouth, since this enabled them to attract British traffic and so compete with the English liners that used the Mersey as base.

The level of rivalry on land equal-led that at sea, since the London & South Western and Great Western Railways both served Plymouth and, in particular, competed for this specialised traffic. The LSWR was at a slight advantage with their passengers, who joined the special trains at Stonehouse Pool. From here they were worked to Devonport where they reached the LSWR main line for the journey to Exeter round the northern edge of Dartmoor. To that point the LSWR route was undoubtedly longer than their rival's steeply-graded direct line across the South Devon via Totnes, but this was still the era when the initials GWR also stood for the Great Way Round, and the overall distance between quayside and London terminus gave the LSWR line to Waterloo an advantage of some 15 miles over the Paddington route. Although the Great Western handled some of the passengers, it was with the mail that it could provide a better overall service, since a proportion of the mailbags were destined for the Midlands and the North of England and could be loaded into a special van which was detatched at Bristol during the train's brief stop there.

1904 was a particularly important year for the Great Western Railway in the West of England. With the traumas of the gauge conversion a dozen years in the past, they were planning to introduce a new seven-hour train between London and Penzance, called the 'Plymouth, Falmouth & Penzance Limited' express, at the start of the summer timetable that year, while work was already in progress with the construction of the missing links in the new direct route via Westbury. The new train's timings included the world's longest scheduled non-stop run in each direction between Paddington and Plymouth, and the new service was to prove so popular that passenger bookings at Penzance increased by no less than 68 per cent. Contempor-ary British railway companies in the 1900s could not afford to miss exploiting any business possibilities of this sort at a time when they were at the peak of their prosperity and influence. The new King (Edward VII) had set his seal of approval on fast railway travel in the first few days of his reign when the funeral train had conveyed the body of Queen Victoria to London at a speed which his late mother would never have countenanced during her lifetime. Royalty had, indeed, positively spurred the GWR on to show what it could do. In July 1903 the Prince and Princess of Wales (later to become King George V and Queen Mary) had made a journey to the West of England, and it had been intimated to the GWR that their Royal Highnesses would like "a good run". The result was spectacular, with Driver Burden at the regulator of *City of Bath* reaching Plymouth no less than 37 minutes early, non-stop, at an average speed of just over 63 mph. It was not only passenger traffic that was booming as British coal production was increasing from 225 million tons in 1900 to 263 million five years later, with the railways playing a vital role in making the country the power-house of the world.

The task of transferring the mails off the *Kronprinz Wilhelm* from Plymouth to Paddington on May 9 1904 was thus a very important business opportunity for the Great Western Railway, and gave their publicity people an admirable opportunity to publicise any fast running. In addition to the gold bullion already mentioned, there were the usual mails from the Un-

Right: Artist George Heiron's impression of No. 3440 *City of Truro* with the up 'Ocean Mail' special of May 9 1904, leaving Whiteball Tunnel at more than 80 mph, and accelerating to a maximum of 102.3 mph, according to Charles Rous-Marten.
Copyright Silver Link Publishing.

ited States which were supplemented by those from Australia and New Zealand which had been transferred by rail across the North American continent from San Francisco. The GWR sent Assistant Superintendent of the Line Mr. C. Aldington to Plymouth to take charge of the whole operation, and Driver Moses Clements from Exeter, a very smart man, was in charge of the first stage of the journey to London. On the footplate with him was Inspector G. H. Flewellen, of Newton Abbot, and No. 3440 *City of Truro*, one of the latest 'City' locomotives, was rostered for the train. This class was popular with the footplate crews, and their exploits had frequently delighted the 'railwayacs' of that period.

Although these ocean mail specials did not carry ordinary passengers, neither of the rival railways missed the resulting opportunities for publicity. The GWR was particularly active in this respect and the first issue of the 'Railway Magazine' for 1904 started with an account by Herbert Russell of 'An American Mail Boat Train on the Great Western Railway'. Two well-known contemporary recorders of train performance were, however, given special facilities to travel on the specials on numerous occasions. They were Charles Rous-Marten and the Rev. W.J. Scott, both of whom were extensive contributors to the railway press in their day and who had even been invited to travel on the Royal Special to Plymouth the previous summer. Back in 1901 Rous-Marten had started the 'British Locomotive Practice and Performance' series in the 'Railway Magazine', which was to turn out to be the longest-running railway column in the world, and Rev. Scott was one of those who took over its authorship after Rous-Marten's death in 1908. Between them they made numerous journeys on the specials in April and May 1904, but it was Rous-Marten who was the privileged recorder behind Driver Clements and *City of Truro* on May 9 1904.

On this occasion the GWR's share of the special traffic was confined solely to mails, the train comprising "five heavily-laden double-bogie eight-wheeled postal vans, one being still a larger sorting van; the total weight, including mails and specie, was estimated at 148 tons exclusive of engine and tender." The transfer of 1,300 mail bags from the *Kronprinz Wilhelm* had been smartly carried out, and the loading arranged so that one of the vans could be detached at Bristol with the mail for the destinations other than London.

Like all such operations in dock areas, the initial stretches were taken very slowly, but *City of Truro*, just a year old, finally got the 'Right Away' at Millbay Dock Crossing just after 9.23 that morning, only 83 minutes after the liner's arrival. The 'Cities' were the final development of Dean's outside-framed 4-4-0s for express passenger duties. The first had appeared in September 1902 when a larger Standard No. 4 boiler had been put on one of the 'Atbara' class, No. 3405, *Mauritius*, and this was followed by the 10 new locomotives (Nos. 3433–3442) all of which were named after cities served by the GWR. With their 'extended wagon-top boilers and Belpaire fireboxes' they looked impressive but not particularly handsome, with nothing more than a tapered cast-iron chimney to complement the brass safety-valve cover. If Swindon were to have fitted one of the copper-capped chimneys, like the one used on the new 4-6-0 No 100 *William Dean*, one could easily see that the result would be a considerable visual improvement. Still 'handsome is as handsome does', and there was certainly nothing wrong with the class when it came to performance on the road with the relatively light expresses of the day. It was clear that there could well be a case for rebuilding some more of the 'Atbaras' to match in a few years' time when their smaller boilers needed renewal, and this was done with nine further 'Atbaras' in the 1907–09 period, which brought the class to a total of 20.

By 9.20 in the morning on May 9 1904 Plymouth was already busy. The morning shoppers were coming into the city on the new trams, as well as the trains, while horses and carts rumbled their way through the streets on their delivery rounds. The special's progress through Plymouth was fairly sedate initially, with the climb and then the triangle to negotiate between Millbay and North Road stations, which took just over three minutes. Then, having reached the main line, there came the sharp climb to Mutley Tunnel. Just before this they ran through the platforms of Mutley station serving the nearby parts of the city. With the increasing travel prompted by the new electric tramways and the rising

prosperity, there were already plans to build a series of similar halts in the Plymouth area where the services were to be worked by the new rail-motors. The first of these halts was already under construction at Lipson Vale on the descent from the tunnel to the Plym estuary at Laira. This incline gave the train its first chance to get moving in earnest, passing Lipson Junction en-route, where the down LSWR trains regained their own metals to run round to Friary station and Sutton Harbour. It was over this stretch that the rival companies' London-bound expresses were actually running in opposite directions!

For any GWR steam-hauled up express it was vital to get going as quickly as possible along the next stretch in order to rush Hemerdon Bank, with its 1 in 42 gradients, which starts only some two miles away, just beyond Plympton station. Driver Clements made good use of the hard work put in by his fireman, reaching 70 mph along the level, and then going up the bank at a sustained 27 mph, Plympton to Hemerdon only taking 3 min. 55 sec. for the 2.6 miles.

They were by this stage well out into the Devonshire countryside with its narrow muddy lanes, now starting to dry out after the rains of the winter. The village road men were at work on the few major roads, spreading, watering and rolling the stone surfacing they had spent the winter preparing. Their wages were met out of the parish rates, and in some of the less-populated areas the railways were probably the largest ratepayers because of the somewhat depressed state of the country's agriculture. Herds of red Devon cattle and flocks of sheep nevertheless dotted the hillsides, while the last of the spring blossom could be seen on the sheltered orchards of the farms and cottages. Only the occasional farm cart rumbled along the roads, although down in Cornwall the GWR had, with great pioneering spirit, introduced their own bus services the previous summer.

After the railway's very steep ascent to Hemerdon, there are still more than 7½ miles to the summit at Wrangaton, all of which was covered with the speed just over the 60 mph mark. They cleared the station there less than 16¾ mins after passing North Road, and then began a very fast descent into Totnes, with speeds in the high 70s. The riding of

Above: The clean lines and Edwardian grace of the 'City' class are shown to good effect in this broadside portrait of No. 3440 *City of Truro* in the unmodified condition in which it is claimed to have achieved 102.3 mph. The rather portly driver, leaning on the handbrake, is standing approximately where the fireman would have stood to feed the fire — a task which must have required great skill and fine balance whilst travelling at the high speeds recorded on the 'Ocean Mail' specials. The cab clearly afforded little protection from the weather to the crew. *GWR Museum, Swindon.*

Above: Dean 'Single' No. 3065 *Duke of Connaught*, the locomotive which replaced *City of Truro* at the head of the up 'Ocean Mail' special at Bristol on May 9 1904 for the final portion of the trip to Paddington. With Driver Underhill at the regulator, the 4-2-2 averaged 80 mph for 73 continuous miles between Swindon and Paddington, including a maximum of 87 mph at Maidenhead. "Such figures," says Rous-Marten, "simply make one gasp." *GWR Museum, Swindon.*

the 'Cities' certainly seems to have inspired confidence with their crews, as the high speeds achieved with *City of Truro* had been closely approached on more than one previous occasion. Totnes was taken at full speed, and a good climb made over the Dainton gable with a minimum of 35 mph, only 5 min. 1 sec. being required for the 4¾ mile ascent. Notwithstanding the ferocious gradients that were a legacy from Brunel's 'Atmospheric Caper', they passed Newton Abbot (31.8 miles from North Road) at "a carefully reduced speed" in 36 min. 42 sec., which takes some doing even with one of today's HSTs. The Ocean Mail special, however, did not have to worry about the passengers' comfort, Rous-Marten doubtless being delighted to record the sparkling performance. After Newton, the

quick dash down the Teign Estuary was followed by a slowing over the reverse curves through the station. Progress along the sea wall below the red sandstone cliffs was not as effortless as it is today, as there were still 1½-miles of single track to negotiate through the five tunnels before Dawlish, with slowings at each end to collect and deliver the tablet. Near Starcross there was a severe permanent-way slowing, but after this they could run fast as far as Exeter. The new water troughs at Exminster were not due to be in service until June for the start of the summer services, so they had to continue for another 38 miles to Creech St Michael before there was the opportunity of refilling the tender. With one of the 'Cities' and a light train, however, this was no problem, as numerous earlier runs

had shown, including the non-stop Royal Train journey of the previous July. The line parallels the Exe estuary and the Exeter Canal over this stretch, and approaches the city over the multiple-arched viaduct at St Thomas. At the south end of this, City Basin Junction marked the divergence of the Exeter Railway's route to Christow, only opened in the previous July.

Exeter St Davids again required the speed to come down to little more than walking pace over the junctions and through the station where the train was once more running in the opposite direction to the rival LSWR's up expresses. The latter approached Exeter from the Crediton direction and used the GWR's metals for a couple of miles from Cowley Bridge Junction to the south end of the station. So fierce was the

Left: Class pioneer No. 3405 *Mauritius* passes Hayes, between West Drayton and Southall, with an up express from Weymouth, circa 1910. The locomotive is seen prior to modification with superheating and top-feed, as fitted to the class in the 1910–12 period. *LPC/Ian Allan Ltd.*

Below: 'City' No. 3433 *City of Bath*, in original condition, but paired with an older pattern Dean tender. In July 1903 this locomotive, with Driver Burden in charge, whisked the Prince and Princess of Wales from Paddington to Plymouth at an average speed of slightly more than 63 mph, running non-stop and arriving 37 minutes ahead of booked time! *LPC/Ian Allan Ltd.*

competition between the two companies, that the GWR very firmly insisted on their legal right to ensure that all LSWR trains actually came to a stand in St David's station. This very effectively stopped them getting any sort of a run at the nasty 1 in 36 bank up to Queen Street station. *City of Truro* passed Exeter St David's in 55 min. 55 sec. from North Road, which represented an average of 55.8 mph, the climbs to Hemerdon and Dainton notwithstanding. Good though this was, the time was not quite so good as *City of Gloucester* had achieved a week earlier, although the latter had not had the Starcross slowing to contend with.

As far as the crew of *City of Truro* was concerned, there were no more severe slowings due before Bristol, and the next 30 miles contained the only possibility of achieving a really high maximum speed. The site of any such attempt had to be the five or so miles of steep descent from Whiteball Tunnel through Wellington, just over the county boundary into Somerset. A moderate climb lasts for some 20 miles from Exeter, concluding with the two miles at 1 in 115 through Burlescombe with its sidings going off northward to the quarries. They averaged almost exactly 60 mph the whole way up to the summit at Whiteball Sidings, but as they went over the top speed started to increase very rapidly indeed. They made a "hurricane descent" of the Wellington Bank, according to Rous-Marten, which was "nearly spoiled, however, by a

check near the station through some foolish platelayers calmly staying on the 'four-foot' when the 'lightning special' was close on them". The footplate crew would undoubtedly have realised they were travelling very fast indeed, but they would not have realised that they were in all probability the first people in the world to drive a wheeled vehicle at 100 mph. In the course of the whirlwind descent of the bank, Rous-Marten had recorded a time of $8^4/_5$ seconds for a quarter mile, which, as it stands, corresponds to a speed of 102 mph, the significance and accuracy of which we will be con-

sidering later in this account. Although the regulator had to be closed and a brake application made because of the platelayers, Driver Clements still managed to run the 10.8 miles from Whiteball Summit to Taunton in 8 min. 20 secs., and had, to that point, averaged 59.3 mph from North Road.

For the rest of *City of Truro*'s run to Bristol the gradients were slight, and the 4-4-0 was able to show its haulage capabilities over virtually level track. The Ocean Mail specials stopped at Pyle Hill, about half a mile short of Temple Meads station, to change locomotives, if necessary,

'Bulldog' 4-4-0 No. 3460 *Montreal* sprints along the sea-front at Teignmouth with a down express in 1908. The 'Bulldog' and 'Atbara' 4-4-0s were identical in many respects, the chief difference being driving wheel diameter. The 'Bulldogs' were fitted with 5ft 8½in diameter wheels against the 6ft 8½in wheels fitted to the 'Atbara' and therefore the 'City' 4-4-0s. *R. Brookman.*

and also to cut off the mail van for the north, and *City of Truro* managed to average 72.7 mph pass-to-stop over this 44.2 mile stretch. Leaving Taunton they would have picked up water from the troughs at Creech St Michael, but these would then have been the last country station of Durston. Today we are used to the flyover at Cogload, but that only dates from 1932, while the present West of England line from there to Castle Cary was not brought into use until July 1906. Prior to that there was only the Bristol & Exeter Railway's branch from Durston to Yeovil via Curry Rivell which had been opened in 1853. As part of its plan for improving the West of England route, the GWR had got Parliamentary authority for a new line from Castle Cary to Curry Rivell in 1896, which was supplemented by the Athelney-Cogload chord which was not actually authorised until three months after *City of Truro*'s record run, although its completion was to occupy less than two years. The final approach to Bristol was also very different in 1904 to what it today, as a result of the changes that

followed the quadrupling carried out between the two World Wars.

The whole run from Plymouth North Road to Pyle Hill occupied just 12 seconds over the even two hours, corresponding to an average of 63.4 mph pass-to-stop, inclusive of the various slowings. To ensure that all went smoothly on this important occasion, the GWR had stand-by locomotives available at five places en-route; Newton Abbot, Exeter, Taunton, Bristol and Swindon. It had been intended that *City of Truro* would work right through to London, but a quick inspection of the tender indicated that it would be touch and go whether the remaining coal, excellent though its quality was, would be enough to get the train to Paddington. It was accordingly decided to use the standby locomotive here, and in less than four minutes the Dean 'Single', No. 3065 *Duke of Connaught*, had replaced the 4-4-0 and was off on its way to London.

Before leaving the events of May 9 1904 we must briefly include the details of the final section of the Ocean Mail special's journey from Bristol to London. The load had been reduced to just four vans, grossing 120 tons, for the remaining 118.4 miles to Paddington. They were hampered by the start being over the Bristol avoiding line past the site of the locomotive depot at St Philip's Marsh that was active until the latter days of steam. It was not until they had negotiated the North Somerset/St Anne's Park triangle that they rejoined the main line to

London and could again get going properly. They were also hampered by a severe slowing over the Cricklade bridge at Swindon, but the subsequent performance of the 'Single' was brilliant. Speeds were in the high seventies or eighties from Uffington to Ealing Broadway with a maximum of 87 mph at Maidenhead, giving an overall time of 99 min. 46 sec. from Pylle Hill, corresponding to an average 71.2 mph. Only 3¾ minutes had been required for the locomotive change at Bristol, so the mails and bullion had been whisked from Millbay Dock Crossing to London in 3 hours 46 min. and 48 sec., which made May 9 1904 one of the most notable dates in the long history of the Great Western Railway.

During the 80-odd years that followed the *City of Truro*'s run from Plymouth to Bristol, the question of the maximum speed achieved has been the subject of much discussion and controversy. We cannot leave this account of the locomotive's exploits, therefore, without considering in greater length the question of what was the maximum speed attained on May 9 1904.

First and foremost there is no way in which we can, at this range, prove anything with the level of accuracy that is now customary for speed records in other fields of endeavour. Sophisticated timing devices are available to time athletic records, while modern track recording vehicles, such as those operated by the Railway Technical Centre at Derby, enable far more accurate figures to be obtained compared with those of Rous-Marten. However, it is still customary for point-to-point railway speed records in this country to be recorded by stop watches, or their modern electronic equivalents, and I have personally been involved as the official recorder on a number of such runs in the last few years. Much though we would like to be able to apply any of these present-day methods to the exploits of *City of Truro*, we cannot go back in time, and we only have the rather scanty information left by Rous-Marten, who died just over four years after the run concerned.

The position is complicated by the fact that although a number of reports about the journey were published immediately after the event, the GWR asked for the details to be 'hushed-up', despite Rous-Marten's wishes to the contrary, only releasing them in 1922. What complicates the situation even further is that it was only after a further 12 years had elapsed that Rous-Marten's figures were called into question. Cecil J. Allen, who was then writing the 'Locomotive Practice & Performance' column in the 'Railway Magazine', devoted considerable space into the subject in several articles in 1934 but unfortunately much of the discussion was not based on the original figures that were available. In 1954, to mark the silver jubilee of the run, O.S. Nock carried out an exhaustive examination of the available figures, and his conclusions were also published in the appendix of his book 'Speed Records on Britain's Railways' (David & Charles 1971). That account, however, did not take into consideration one limitation of the recording methods used in Rous-Marten's days which can provide an important insight into our problem. As the current author of the 'Railway Magazine's' 'Locomotive Practice & Performance' I was able to deal with this point in my April 1983 article when I paid tribute to Rous-Marten's work on the occasion of the 75th anniversary of his death.

When considering the accuracy of any log, one must inevitably take into account the standing of the recorder. In this connection Rous-Marten's reputation is one that many of us would envy. A few years ago Professor Jack Simmons kindly provided me with some biographical notes on Rous-Marten, which form the basis of the information that follows. Rous-Marten was born in 1844, and, with his family, emigrated to New Zealand 15 years later. He followed a journalistic career, but had numerous interests. At one time he possessed what was believed to be the largest musical library in the Southern Hemisphere, and a paper of his on the 1885 eclipse of the sun was read to the Royal Astronomical Society. When he was 43 years old the New Zealand Government asked him to undertake a study of the railways of Britain, and the subsequent report attracted great interest in many parts of the world. After that he was commissioned to prepare similar surveys on the railway systems of a number of other countries. The French Government even wanted to award him the Legion of Honour, but he declined this in case it was thought that the standard of his reporting might be influenced as a

The interior of Reading West signal box in the early years of this century. As Charles Rous-Marten reported in 'The Railway Magazine' for June 1904: "The road was kept absolutely clear from first to last," during the May 9 'Ocean Mail' run, and it is likely that men like these were under strict instructions not to impede the paths of these prestige workings. *P. Churchill Collection.*

result. A contemporary writer said "his absolutely impartial method of recording facts made him a *persona grata* to all railway men". It would thus have been completely out of character for him, at the age of 60, suddenly to produce figures that were not of the highest possible standard, bearing in mind too that some of the times would, in any case, be recorded separately by the guard. The Assistant Superintendent of the Line was also highly interested in the progress of the train and may well have been consulting him from time to time.

The maximum speed claimed by Rous-Marten was 102.3 mph, but one must, straight away, say that such a figure cannot be substantiated. Quoting the speed in that way implies that it was 102.3 rather than 102.2 or 102.4 mph, which would mean that there were no errors greater than 1 in 1000. Such an accuracy is quite impossible to achieve with any recordings of the mileposts made from a moving train. Quite apart from the errors inherent in the physical aspects of observing the milepost and pressing the button, the stop-watch could not be read to 1 part in 1000, and we cannot guarantee that there is less than 15 inches error in the positions of consecutive mileposts. At the best, therefore, we can only hope to indicate what *City of Truro*'s maximum speed was to the nearest whole number.

Before looking into the limitations of stop-watches, however, there are

a number of other more-general points that should be discussed. There is, first of all, the question of whether a steam locomotive in 1904 could possibly attain a speed of 100 mph or thereabouts. It was not until a further 30 years had passed before anything similar was achieved in this country, and even then the record of LNER A1 'Pacific' No. 4472 *Flying Scotsman* is not without some degree of controversy. Railway speed records are traditionally not attained on level track but on a downgrade, which means that gravity plays a large part in the achievements. Down from Whiteball Tunnel there are 2½-miles inclined at 1 in 80/90 after which the gradients ease out to 1 in 133 before, and 1 in 170 after Wellington station. Railway coaching vehicles will run away at very high speeds down such inclines, and using the Johansen formula for train resistance developed by the LMS in the 1930s, it can be shown that the terminal speed for coaching stock on 1 in 90 is of the order of 105 mph and is still as high as 80 mph on the 1 in 133. So to achieve such speeds down these gradients, all the locomotive has to do is to exert enough power to keep itself ahead of the coaches. While the 1904 mail vans were undoubtedly 'dirtier' aerodynamically than the LMS stock of the 1930s, the specific resistance figures have been applied to the whole trailing load and not just to the tare weights, which provides at least some degree of compensation. No great power output by the locomotive would thus have been required on Wellington Bank to maintain a speed of 100 mph.

An equally important factor in assessing *City of Truro*'s performance is whether it was possible to accelerate sufficiently fast to achieve the speed in the distance available. The power/weight ratio provides a useful indication of the acceleration likely to be achieved by any particular train. At speeds in the 90–100 mph range down gradients of the sort we are discussing, gravity itself provides a very high proportion of the overall power/weight ratio. Together with the locomotive and tender, the weight of the Ocean Mail special was 240 tons, and at 95 mph on the 1 in 80 and 1 in 90 gradients, gravity would provide the equivalent of 1,700 and 1,500 horsepower respectively. It is not as easy to calculate the potential maximum power output from a 'City' at the same speed, but we can, nevertheless, at least try and make a sensible estimate. In the first of the BR Test Bulletins to be published after Nationalisation, one of the Hawksworth 'Hall' 4-6-0s achieved a very flat maximum indicated horsepower output of 1,450 over the speed range 50–70 mph. This corresponded to 53.7 horsepower per square foot of grate area, and was achieved with the locomotive being on a grate limit. So if *City of Truro* was similarly restricted on Wellington Bank one

would expect an indicated output of approximately 1,100 horsepower. The 4-4-0 was, however, bereft of superheating, piston valves and many other modern developments, so perhaps we should reduce the figure by a third to 725 horsepower, which coincides closely with the 730 hp measured at 68 mph with the 'Duke' class 4-4-0 *Amyas* in 1897. Combining this with the effects of gravity gives us 2,400 available horsepower on 1 in 80, dropping to 2,200 on the 1 in 90.

The corresponding power/weight ratios for the 1904 special train then work out at 10.0 and 9.2 respectively. Thanks to modern-day technology we now have a ready means of putting these figures in proportion, as we can look at the corresponding ones for an HST. The pair of 'Valentas' in its power cars produce a total of 4,500 horsepower, but when train heating and other losses are provided for, the rail horsepower is only in the range 3,250–3,600 horsepower. For a fully-loaded '2 + 7' formation these figures in turn correspond to a power/weight ratio in the range 8.0–8.9. Down Wellington Bank, therefore, the Ocean Mail special would have had an acceleration that was fractionally better than the figures that one of today's Western Region HSTs can achieve on the level.

When I was in the cab of the 'Cornish Riviera' leaving Paddington in the summer of 1983, we

accelerated from 97 mph to 104 mph in a mile up a gradient of 1 in 1,204 through Ealing Broadway with the air-conditioning working flat-out and the kitchen preparing for lunch. This is a very sweeping comparison but it does enable us to appreciate *City of Truro*'s dynamics as it charged down Wellington Bank in 1904.

The sequence of quarter-mile timings left us by Rous-Marten were apparently made with a pair of fifth-second stop-watches. From the exit of Whiteball Tunnel they were as follows, the second line giving the corresponding speeds to the nearest whole mile per hour:

11, $10^3/_5$, $10^1/_5$, 10, $9^4/_5$, $9^2/_5$, $9^1/_5$, $8^4/_5$ secs
82, 85, 88, 90, 92, 96, 98, 102 mph

Over each full mile the speed increases are 8, 7, 10 and 12 mph, which are very definitely in the wrong direction because the gradients over this particular stretch are easing from 1 in 80 to 1 in 90. While curvature and wind might produce small differences, they are unlikely to give such a pattern, and, in particular, it is the last quarter that seems so to be badly out of sequence. It is thus highly likely that the speed of 102 mph is incorrect. So we have to conclude that *City of Truro* did *not* attain such a maximum down Wellington Bank in 1904.

What then was the probable maximum speed on this never-to-be-forgotten occasion? This is where we have to consider the workings of the stop-watch. The hands of such an instrument do not rotate at a constant angular velocity, as the mechanism moves in a series of jerks with each release of the escapement as the balance wheel swings. The periodicity of this is dependent on the minimum intervals it is required to measure with the watch, and it is not possible to improve the accuracy of the readings simply by using a magnifiying glass. The actual movement of the hands only requires about 1 or 2 thousandths of a second, so if one finds that the watch has been stopped half-way between two successive marks on the dial, the elapsed time is still effectively that corresponding to the longer interval. It is thus entirely possible that Rous-Marten's watch was within 0.002 seconds of the full 9 sec. when he pressed the button for the last of the readings quoted. This corresponds to a speed of 100 mph exactly, and the acceleration over the final full mile drops to 10 mph. O.S. Nock's analysis came to

In immaculate condition, No. 3436 *City of Chester* rests between duties at Westbourne Park shed, circa 1904. *LPC/Ian Allan Ltd.*

the same conclusion without, however, providing an explanation for the way in which the final reading could have been wrong. There is one other slight discrepancy in Rous-Marten's figures, and that concerns the time between Whiteball and Wellington. It is obvious that he had to obtain his passing times in a totally different way to those used to record the speed, and with all the excitement of the fast running and the drama of the platelayers it would be only too easy to record the wrong figure for this. It should also be remembered that within seconds of passing Whiteball signal box they would have plunged into the darkness of the tunnel and we do not know how good the lighting was in the vans. For my money, therefore, there is a strong presumption that in 1904 'City of Truro' became the first vehicle in the world to achieve a speed of 100 mph.

There are, however, one or two other points just worth considering in conclusion. First of all, what were the platelayers doing and what effect did they have on the running? Clearly at the speed that had been attained, Driver Clements did not have the slightest chance of stopping the train clear of the gang had they not stepped out of the 'four-foot' at the last moment. Why, however, were they there, and why did they not do anything to acknowledge the frantic whistling? It was disconcerting enough when I was riding on the front of a diesel locomotive in Chile in April 1985 to have a group of track workers keep going back to tinker with the rails as we fought our way towards them across the Atacama Desert, flat-out up the grades at 11 kilometres per hour! How much more worrying must the actions of the Somerset gang have appeared to those on *City of Truro* which was, in any case, going faster than anyone aboard had ever been before. It would have needed an almost foolhardy display of bravado not to shut the regulator and apply the brake in such circumstances. Rous-Marten referred to Driver Clements as "a very smart man". He was certainly smart enough to know when to ease up on Wellington Bank.

When all the events of May 9 1904 are taken into consideration, it is unlikely that they included a pre-planned attempt on the world speed record. Earlier, while the track was being upgraded, and whilst other aspects of the organisation for these specials were being sorted out, GWR Chief Mechanical Engineer George Jackson Churchward had given Inspector Flewellen instructions to hold any attempt at a maximum speed record until he gave the word — "after that, you can go and break your bloody neck!" reputedly being the words used! The presence (and persistence) of the permanent way men on the track at Wellington would indicate that important improvements were still in progress and it is probable that the 100 mph record was not planned from the outset. The footplate crew was undoubtedly out to put up as good a run as possible, but when they let the locomotive have its head down the bank, the results in all likelihood surprised even them.

Another query is: why was the speed of 100 mph not repeated in Britain for over 30 years? This is undoubtedly tied up with the fact that the GWR authorities must have been really alarmed at what had happened, and hastily took steps to have the full details 'hushed-up' until the passage of time and the development of technology made a figure of 100 mph not appear so frightening to the general public. There was, nevertheless still some more fast running on the Wellington Bank and Rous-Marten quoted a speed of 95 mph in one of his 1906 articles. Finding the limits of safety with railway speeds was certainly not a particularly precise art in 1904, and one could not very well run trains at steadily increasing speeds over a particular section of line until one actually came off. It should not be forgotten that, only eight years earlier, there had been a disastrous high-speed derailment at Preston less than 12 months after the 1895 'Races to the North'. That was warning enough, but on July 1 1906, the day the GWR opened its Castle Cary route to the West of England, one of the LSWR up Ocean Liner Expresses spread itself across the tracks at Salisbury as it came through that station too fast. I have a suspicion too that a comparatively light 4-4-0 rode better than a later 4-6-0 or 'Pacific', at least until track standards had recovered from the effects of World War I and had been improved during the 1930s to handle the faster services. This could help explain the reluctance of later drivers to run as fast as Driver Clements did, even when they had bigger and more powerful locomotives. It is also possible that the outside frames of 'Cities' might just have given them marginally more stability. There is always some friction between an axlebox and its guides, which adds to the shock-absorbing effect of the locomotive's leaf springs. Because of the longer moment arm on an outside-framed locomotive, this would reduce any tendency to roll rather more than it would with the frames in their more-usual inside position. It is of interest to record that on most of the contemporary four-coupled locomotives, certainly those that have been preserved, the driving axles are provided with helical rather than leaf springs. These provide far less damping of the irregularities in the track, as one can appreciate particularly with LNWR 2-4-0 No. 790 *Hardwicke*, (built 1892) both of whose coupled axles have helical springs.

To sum up a long story, therefore, we cannot be entirely certain precisely what was the maximum speed that *City of Truro* achieved during its whirlwind descend of Wellington Bank in May 1904, but even if we cannot substantiate a speed of 102.3 mph, there are strong indications that it did just reach 100 mph, thus deservedly earning its special place in history. Whatever the maximum speed was, the whole run was an absolute triumph for the GWR and did much to establish the company's image in popular esteem. We must not, however, forget *Duke of Connaught*'s contribution to the success of the day, and breathe a sigh of regret that we are not also able to get that locomotive out of a museum to participate in the 1985 celebrations. Perhaps for the centenary of the great day in 2004 we can persuade someone to put a J94 boiler inside *The Queen* at Windsor and make the other changes necessary to enable us to see a Dean 'Single' at work alongside *City of Truro*!

CHAPTER 3:

'CITY OF TRURO' AT WORK: 1903–1931

Keith M. Beck

ON A September day in 1902 'Atbara' class 4-4-0 No. 3405 *Mauritius* re-emerged from Swindon Works after being re-boilered with Churchward's new Standard No. 4 boiler. Its new boiler was not only larger in diameter, but the rear portion was tapered so that it rose to meet the outline of the firebox; however, there was little to indicate that the new boiler was the true prototype of the most famous range of boilers in locomotive history, or that *Mauritius* had become the prototype of a class of engines, the '3700's or 'Cities', whose fame would become world-wide.

The boiler carried by *Mauritius*

was the first taper boiler to be borne by a GWR engine and was coned for two-thirds of its length, increasing from 4ft 10¾in at the parallel front ring to no less than 5ft 5in at the firebox tubeplate. Apart from the larger boiler, *Mauritius* had another significant, though not obvious difference from the other 'Atbaras', in that its boiler pressure was raised to 200 psi, compared with it's predecessor's 180 psi. Apart from solitary express passenger 4-6-0 No. 100 (the prototype 'Saint', later named *Dean*, and subsequently *William Dean*) *Mauritius* was the most powerful express engine then running on the GWR.

Within six months No. 3433, the first of 10 new engines, had emerged from Swindon, contemporaneously with a second express passenger 4-6-0 (No. 98) in March 1903. No. 98 was the GWR's second 4-6-0, but it was the first absolutely Standard Churchward design and was thus the precursor of the entire family of Swindon-built two-cylinder 4-6-0s which followed it over the years. On

Below: No. 3714 *City of Gloucester* leaves Paddington during the post-1922 period with a four-coach train, probably for Oxford and Worcester. This locomotive spent the 1920s working from Oxford, Leamington and Worcester before being scrapped on November 23 1929. *Lens of Sutton.*

Right: No. 3441 *City of Winchester* heads a train of clerestory-roofed stock at Hayes, circa 1912, shortly after rebuilding with superheating and top-feed and immediately prior to renumbering as 3718. At this time the locomotive was allocated to Old Oak Common. *LPC/Ian Allan Ltd.*

Below: No. 3437 *City of Gloucester*, circa 1910. The engine is as yet unsuperheated, but retains an old-type Dean railed tender — rather a late survivor. No. 3437 is also still fitted with its original Dean bogie, which had swing-links rather than a central pin to secure it to the locomotive. The Dean bogies were distinguished by the two mountings visible below the bogie side frame. *L&GRP, courtesy David & Charles.*

both Nos. 98 and 3433 the Belpaire firebox had sides which curved very slightly inwards towards the top, and which sloped down slightly towards the cab (the firebox on *Mauritius* had vertical parallel sides). No. 3433 entered traffic without a name, but was soon fitted with nameplates carrying the name *City of Bath*: when, two months later, the remaining nine engines appeared, all were named after cities served by the GWR.

The names ran alphabetically from Bath to Winchester, but the final engine, No. 3442, received the name *City of Exeter*. It has been suggested that this was originally intended to have been *City of Worcester*, but it was decided that this 'faithful city' could be satisfied by its name being already borne by

the Dean 'Single' No. 3027 *Worcester*. As the 'Camel' class 4-4-0 No. 3357 was named *Exeter*, it might have been thought that the citizens of that Devonshire city, not forgetting the Dean and Chapter, would also have been quite content — until it is realised that No. 3440 was *City of Truro* and named after an upstart Cornish city whose cathedral was a mere 25 years old!

The new-build 'Cities' differed in one respect from *Mauritius*, in that the Stroudley pattern of wheel balancing used on the 'Armstrongs', 'Badmintons' and 'Atbaras' was abandoned in favour of the normal method in which the outside cranks were placed diametrically opposite those inside.

The works numbers of the 'Cities' were Nos. 1993–2002, with the

'milestone' number 2000 being borne by the engine which was destined two years later to erect another milestone in locomotive history while descending Wellington Bank at a record-setting speed. That *City of Truro* was originally No. 3440 is universally known; that its worksplate carried the number 2000 is less commonly appreciated. The GWR never paid any attention to such trivia — at least officially! However, one is prompted to wonder if it was just a mere co-incidence that Swindon Works No. 2000 was to establish the 'record of records' — especially when it is realised that at the time of the Wellington Bank 'sprint', at least two other engines of the class, Nos. 3433 *City of Bath* and 3442 *City of Exeter* were reputed to be the fastest of the 'Cities'.

Not only did *City of Bath* enter service at the same time as Churchward's first taper-boilered 4-6-0, No. 98, but later in that momentous year *La France*, a French-built, four-cylinder De Glehn Compound 'Atlantic', arrived on the GWR; while by the end of the year a further 4-6-0, No. 171, had emerged from Swindon. The 'Cities' worked turn and turn about with these much larger engines. However, there was a strong disposition to use the 'Cities' when an assignment of very special importance arose. As O.S. Nock has truly remarked: "No class of British express passenger locomotive — not even the Gresley A4 Pacifics of the LNER — had a more spectacular debut than that of the Great Western 'Cities'".

The visit of the Prince and Princess of Wales to Cornwall in July 1903 saw their three Royal saloons attached to the first portion of the 10-40 am 'Cornishman', which was run *non-stop* to Plymouth, *City of Bath* being used. The engine and Driver Burden were both from Westbourne Park shed, and Burden had already been responsible for some notable runs. With a load of 130 tons gross, No. 3433 ran the 106.9 miles to Bath in 92 min. 02 sec., the 90 miles between Langley and Bath being covered at an average speed of 72 mph with a maximum speed of 81.3 mph at Chippenham. Further west, the section from Nailsea to Durston was run at an average speed of 74 mph; while the journey concluded with some remarkable climbing of the South Devon banks, the minimum speeds being 32 mph at Dainton bank and 36 mph upgrade at Rattery. It was little wonder that the train arrived at Plymouth (North Road) somewhat ahead of schedule — a mere 37 minutes — the overall 246 miles having been run at an average speed of 63.2 mph!

This took place on July 14, less than a fortnight prior to a test run with Churchward's new dynamometer car behind No. 3435 *City of Bristol* between Taunton and Exeter on July 27. The load of 24 tons was considerably heavier than the normal for a GWR express train of that period. The ascent of the steepest part of the Wellington bank was quite exceptional for that time, with the 1 in 80 gradient being topped at 38 mph. One wonders if anyone in the dynamometer car speculated what speed might be achieved by a 'City' unleashed in the reverse direction!

The 'Cities' entered service when the West of England main line was still the 'Great Way Round' via Bristol, where engines were normally changed — except on the handful of Exeter non-stop trains. As it was the practice to also change engines at Exeter, with the 'Dukes' and 'Camels' normally being used west of that point, the 'Cities' rarely appeared in normal circumstances on the most difficult section between Newton Abbot and Plymouth. However, this practice was considerably affected by the introduction of the new express, subsequently known as the 'Cornish Riviera' express, non-stop between Paddington and Plymouth, and during the first few months it was the 'Cities' and 'Frenchies' which were in charge of these workings. For a few months *City of Birming-*

Above: In the typically clean condition of the era, No. 3440 *City of Truro* stands in original condition just outside Paddington, between turns of duty. It is of interest to note that the same footplate crew is visible in the photograph on page 13. *LPC/Ian Allan Ltd.*

The 10.36 London express pauses at Knowle station on March 25 1915 behind No. 3711 *City of Birmingham*. *H. W. Burman.*

Right: An ex-Birmingham train near Oxford heads for Paddington behind No. 3714 *City of Gloucester*, probably in 1922. The picture was certainly taken shortly after the GWR reverted from crimson lake to chocolate and cream livery for its coaches in that year. The leading coach is clearly newly repainted. *L&GRP, courtesy David & Charles.*

ham and *City of Exeter* were shedded at Plymouth.

The 'Cities' had the misfortune to be the last of their line, apart from the smaller-boilered engines of the 'Flower' class 4-4-0s built in 1908. Although many hundreds of engines which carried the No. 4 boiler were to be built in the future, they would be of a very different design. The next lot of 4-4-0s to emerge from Swindon, between May and October 1904, were the outside cylinder 'Counties', Nos. 3473–82. By this time, another 4-4-0 had been rebuilt with the Standard No. 4 boiler, this being the 'Badminton' class engine No. 3310 *Waterford* (originally built in January 1899 with the second prototype No. 2 boiler), which was rebuilt in November 1903.

The summer of 1903 saw the acceleration of some of the best trains between Paddington and Bristol, with the newly-opened Badminton line being used as the route for some of them. The Up 'Flying Dutchman' (8-30 am from Plymouth) was routed via the Badminton line, with a non-stop schedule of 2 hr between Temple Meads and Paddington; while prior to the introduction of the 'Riviera' in the summer of 1904, the 10-45 am from Paddington ran to Bristol in 2 hr 5 min., slipping carriages at Bath. The 'Cities' were used on some of these workings, taking loads of up to 230 tons, which were much heavier than those of the

Royal record run or of the Ocean Mail specials.

A fortnight before the celebrated Ocean Mails run of May 9 1904, *City of Truro* (with the same driver, Moses Clements) on the 12-07 pm up Torquay express — the forerunner of the 'Torquay Express' — which ran non-stop from Exeter, took 209 minutes for the 193.6 miles with a load of 260 tons. On the same train, *City of Exeter*, with 230 tons, took 200 minutes — averaging 75 mph from Wantage Road to Didcot and running at between 70 and 72 mph between Maidenhead and Slough.

However, the 'Counties', 'Atlantics' and Churchward 4-6-0s were soon pressing hard on the heels of

the 'Cities', so that they only enjoyed their prestige role for a couple of years and while a few remained in the West of England until 1912–3, the last to be shedded at Newton Abbot was *City of Truro*, which moved away in August 1913, though No. 3709 *Quebec* remained at Exeter until 1915. The latter was one of a further nine 'Atbaras' rebuilt as 'Cities' between 1907 and 1909: with that orderly mind so rightly associated with the GWR, the engines concerned were Nos. 3400–9 (*Mauritius* being No. 3405). In addition to *Waterford*, another 15 'Badmintons' were similarly rebuilt with No. 4 boilers during 1905–6, and a final one, No. 3293 *Barrington* was done in March 1910; shortly afterwards, the process was reversed and all had been reconverted by 1913. During the time they carried the No. 4 boilers the engines ranked as being temporary members of the 'City' class.

From 1905 the 'Cities' appeared on the Birmingham services — at that time still routed via Oxford — and were working as far north as Chester by 1909. The rebuilt 'Atbaras' were also used on the Wolverhampton line and on the South Wales expresses, being shedded at Cardiff, Landore, Goodwick and even at Carmarthen! The only one in the West of England was No. 3407 *Malta*; while No. 3401 *Gibraltar* spent many years working from Hereford. Though the 'Cities' tenure of the South Wales expresses was

No. 3717 *City of Truro* in later condition, with top-feed, superheating and De-Glehn type bogie. This bogie design, introduced as standard in 1907 with the 'Star' 4-6-0s was added to other classes when they became due for repair. The De Glehn bogie had a central pin, with side-control by springs and side-bearers in place of Dean's swing links. *Lens of Sutton.*

Right: An express comprised entirely of crimson lake liveried stock leaves Paddington behind No. 3715 *City of Hereford*, on an unrecorded date. The GWR discontinued the cream upper panels for coach stock circa 1908 on grounds of cost, and adopted an all-chocolate livery, later changed to crimson lake. Chocolate and cream was re-adopted in 1922. In fact GWR stock had originally been all chocolate, the cream only being added from 1860. *LPC/Ian Allan Ltd.*

Below: A motley selection of stock passes Studley in 1921 with 3716 *City of London* in charge. The train is carrying express headlamps and may have been a theatre special. *L&GRP, courtesy David & Charles.*

not destined to be a lengthy one — the 'Counties' soon replacing them — one of them, No. 3408 *Ophir*, had the honour of inaugurating the Killarney Day Express, with its non-stop run over 261.4 miles between Paddington and Fishguard Harbour in the summer of 1907. The engine was renamed *Killarney* for the occasion, and retained this name for the remainder of its existence. The last two 'Cities' left Cardiff in 1915, for Worcester.

The opening of the new route to Birmingham, via Bicester, saw the 'Cities' sharing in working the new service and they were still engaged on that work in 1913 when *City of Birmingham* was, most appropriate-ly, one of the regular performers. Another new route on which they were used was that between Birmingham and Bristol, via the North Warwickshire line and Honeybourne. They were also employed on the 'North to West' route from Shrewsbury, especially during the war years — though, in this case, the 'Counties' got in first! Their last long distance express working was on the Oxford and Worcester line, which continued into the 1920s.

Superheating was applied to the class between June 1910 and June 1912, *City of Truro* being done in September 1911, when top-feed boiler water supply was also fitted. Shortly afterwards, the 'Cities', in common with the majority of GWR, 4-4-0s, were renumbered: the rebuilt 'Atbaras', hitherto Nos. 3400–9 became Nos. 3700–9; while the 'Cities' exchanged Nos. 3433–42 for Nos. 3710–9, *City of Truro* becoming No. 3717. Its old number, 3440, was given to a 'Bulldog' (formerly No. 3730): one wonders if its crew were ever tempted to 'have a go' in honour of the number's previous owner!

The external appearance of the class had changed somewhat, the cast-iron chimneys originally fitted having been replaced by the built-up pattern with copper caps between 1907 and 1909, those fitted to the 'Cities' having a smaller external diameter than those on other classes. The smokeboxes were also lengthened shortly before the engines were superheated. Previously, between 1904 and 1906, the frames had been strengthened with extra plates, enlarged sand boxes being fitted at about the same time. In common with most of Dean's larger tender engines, all the class were originally fitted with steam reversing gear which many retained throughout their lives and only a few engines appear to have had this replaced by screw reverse, including *City of Truro*. A later change was the provision of piston valves in place of the original slide valves; however, this did not commence until May 1915. *City of Truro*, by now No. 3717, was fitted with piston valves in November 1915. The first few tenders attached had coal rails, but

Left: A stopping train comprised of LMS stock leaves Shrewsbury for Hereford, circa 1925, hauled by No. 3708 *Killarney*. This locomotive was named *Ophir* until September 1907. *LPC/Ian Allan Ltd.*

Below: No. 3717 *City of Truro* pauses at Shrewsbury station in August 1930, the same month that approaches were made to the LNER with the aim of placing the locomotive in the old York Railway Museum. *National Railway Museum.*

these were superseded by plate fenders: the original tenders were of 3,000 gallons capacity, but some engines later ran with 3,500 gallon tenders.

City of Truro received new cylinders in 1907 (at 187,184 miles), a second new set when piston valves were fitted (at 522,489 miles), and yet another set in March 1922 (at 725,929 miles): records show that the engine constantly showed slightly more wear in the right-hand cylinder than in the left! The superheated boiler fitted in 1911 was the sixth boiler which the engine had carried: the original (B.3429) was replaced in March 1906, another was fitted in October 1907; while the engine received two new boilers in 1909 — in March and October respectively. Further boiler exchanges were made in 1915 (when piston valve cylinders were fitted), 1920, 1921, 1925 and 1928. The engine's weight appears to have varied at each weighing, ranging from 55 tons 9 cwt to 57 tons 14 cwt between November 1915 and October 1925!

The total mileage run prior to withdrawal was 1,000,483 miles. The annual mileage prior to superheating in 1911 averaged 44,900 miles; during the next 14 years the average was 36,000 mles a year — though between July 1923 and August 1925, when working mostly from Banbury shed, the mileage was 88,228 miles; between 1925 and 1928 it was at an annual rate of 37,000 miles; and it was only during its final three years that it dropped appreciably, to 21,000 miles. What is surprising is the amount of time the engine spent idle while under repair, an average of 67 days per annum during its 28 years of service — this

included some quite extended periods in Swindon Works, such as 108 days in 1905–6, 114 in 1911 (when superheated), 105 days in 1913, 155 days in 1915 (piston valves fitted), 231 days in 1920, 166 days in 1922 and 199 days in 1928.

The latter days saw the 'Cities' reduced to second-rate work: *Killarney* was no longer running non-stop from Paddington to Fishguard and it was many years since *City of Truro* had run at over 100 mph: both engines were to be found working local trains from Shrewsbury. The 'writing was on the wall' when *City of Winchester* was withdrawn in October 1927 and by 1931 only two of the class remained at work, Nos. 3712 *City of Bristol* and 3717 *City of Truro*. Although the former engine was to enjoy the melancholy distinction of being the last 'City' to be withdrawn, *City of Truro* was spared from destruction.

In August 1930 approaches were

made to the LNER for the engine to find a resting place in the York Railway Museum. The Secretary of the Museum wrote to LNER Assistant General Manager Robert Bell at Kings Cross: "I saw Mr Boyd-Carpenter at Doncaster yesterday. Apparently he is a friend of Mr Collett, Chief Mechanical Engineer of the Great Western Railway. His story is that Mr Collett has told him that if he can find a permanent home for the "City of Truro" engine, which is shortly to be out of traffic, he is at liberty to do so. I think the real position is that we are being sounded in this round-about way as to whether we would accept the engine if offered . . ."

The Railway Museum and the LNER both reacted favourably to this suggestion and a fascinating correspondence followed (reproduced in full in Appendix 3, page 45) between York, Kings Cross and Paddington, regarding the future of

Above: Class prototype No. 3705 Mauritius, pictured at Pangbourne towards the end of its life in the late 1920s with a down Didcot slow train. *L&GRP, courtesy David & Charles.*

Right: A long way from home. No. 3717 is prepared to travel the last few feet into the York Railway Museum in March 1931. *National Railway Museum.*

Below right: Into retirement. Polished to perfection, *City of Truro* **stands in silent display in the old York Railway Museum. Who would have dreamed it would be recalled to service on two further occasions?** *National Railway Museum.*

City of Truro.

The GWR agreed to let the locomotive go to York, and while General Manager J. Milne at one stage claimed that he 'did not consider the engine to be of outstanding importance', he added that the 4-4-0 should remain at the disposal of the GWR if it wished to use it for any purpose at any stage in the future.

Thus *City of Truro* entered what was anticipated would be its final and permanent resting place. It was appropriate that the engine which had made such unexpected history on May 9 1904 should later create further unexpected history by emerging from the Museum at York in 1957 and once again run over that very same line on which it had achieved the 'record of records' over half-a-century before.

Finally, it is interesting to note from Swindon Works engine records, now lodged with the National Railway Museum, that No. 3440 *City of Truro*, built in 1903 at a cost of £1,957, had a 'written down' value of just £235 at the time of its withdrawal and presentation to the York Railway Museum!

Top: With three years of running on its record card since removal from the old York Railway Museum, No. 3440 *City of Truro* **is prepared for duty at Eastleigh shed on a clear spring day on May 14 1960.** *W. Potter.*

Above: A Stephenson Locomotive Society special hauled by No. 3440 *City of Truro* **runs between Reading and Tilehurst in the summer of 1960.** *Dr. J. A. Coiley.*

CHAPTER 4:

OUT OF RETIREMENT: 1957–1962

R.C. Riley

RIGHT from the onset of the Nationalisation of British Railways on January 1 1948 the Western Region showed a marked degree of independence. Indeed on the very last day of 1947, on the very eve of Nationalisation, the GWR ordered 200 of the 94xx Class 0-6-0PT's from outside contractors. These locomotives were not all delivered until 1956, by which time they were already starting to become surplus to requirements.

In July 1955 a new Chairman was appointed to the Western Region Board, Reginald F. Hanks, a man imbued with the GWR tradition: he had trained at Swindon and then spent some time in the motor industry before joining the WR. This was two years after the 1953 Transport Act, which abolished the Railway

Executive and gave greater authority to the Regions — and the late Reginald Hanks took great advantage of this. Up to that time only 'Kings', 'Castles' and 'Stars' were painted in lined green. The 'Saints', 'Counties' and 'Halls' had to run in mixed traffic lined black livery, all other engines being painted in unlined black. In 1955 however, a tentative start was made by Hanks in extending the lined Brunswick green livery to 'Counties' and 'Modified Halls' and in the following year two Churchward 2-6-0's appeared in lined green, ostensibly for a Royal train duty. The principle thus established, there then followed the painting in lined green of just about every engine likely to work a passenger train — down to 56xx Class 0-6-2Ts and 14xx Class 0-4-2Ts! Even BR

Heading a three-coach Southampton – Newbury train on May 25 1957, No. 3440 *City of Truro* runs under clear signals as it approaches Swaythling. *E.R. Morten.*

Standard engines emerged in Brunswick green. Named trains had their carriage stock repainted in the once familiar chocolate and cream, with several additional trains being named to provide the excuse for repainting even more coaches in the old colours of 'the Company', as the GWR was invariably known to its staff.

This was the atmosphere of revived Great Westernry into which Churchward 4-4-0 *City of Truro* (still carrying its last GWR number — 3717) emerged from the old York Museum in January 1957 and was

Above: *City of Truro* reverted from its last GWR number 3717 to its original number 3440 in 1957 to avoid confusion with '5700' 0-6-0PT No. 3717, one of a batch of locomotives introduced in 1933, two years after *City of Truro*'s withdrawal. *F.K. Davies.*

Above right: It's February 3 1957 and *City of Truro* is stripped for overhaul in Swindon Works' 'A' shop. *Eric Mountford.*

Right: *City of Truro* undergoes valve-setting at Swindon works, February 22 1957. *BR/OPC.*

sent to Swindon Works for overhaul, a hitherto unprecedented move. Perhaps Hanks was aware of the terms under which the locomotive had gone to York in 1931, and invoked Swindon's dormant claim to the locomotive. (See appendix 3) Since *City of Truro* carried a Standard No. 4 superheated boiler there was no problem in reboilering it in the main Erecting Shop. It had carried in its latter GWR years the number 3717 and the more austere plain green livery during its stay in York Museum, with the words 'Great Western' on the tender sides, to conform with its superheated rebuilding. In 1957 however it was repainted in the attractive and elaborate 1903 livery and reverted to its old No. 3440, the reason for this being to prevent any confusion with 0-6-0PT No. 3717, which was stationed at Pontypool Road.

Thus it emerged from Swindon Works in a state of Edwardian elegance and was temporarily housed in the Stock Shed. Before the end of March it was doing the usual Swindon running-in turns; stopping trains to and from Didcot, Bath or Bristol. The intention was to run it on suitable service trains, at the same time making it available to work special trains. In fact its first special train was worked for the AGM of the Festiniog Railway Preservation Society at Portmadoc, on March 30, when it ran from Paddington to Ruabon and back. Then the decision was taken to allocate *City of Truro* to Didcot, where it regularly worked service trains over the Didcot, Newbury and Southampton line, often outward on the 12.42 pm Didcot and back on the 4.56 pm Southampton.

On April 23 No. 3440 worked a special from Pontypridd to Swindon, via Radyr, Waterhall Junction and Cardiff. Outwards the schedule was an easy one, 67½ miles in 105 minutes, but on the return journey Cardiff was reached in under 100 minutes with a maximum of 80 mph at Little Somerford.

The next tour, the RCTS, 'North Somerset Rail Tour' of April 28 1957, was more ambitious. The seven-coach/240 tons train was hauled from Waterloo to Reading over an unusual route, via Weybridge, Virginia Water West Curve and Reading Old Junction, by No. 30453 *King Arthur*. At Reading *City of Truro* came on and Reginald Hanks was on the platform to see the train off and was clearly delighted at the sight. Starting over the Berks. & Hants. Line, the train continued via Westbury, Bradford-on-Avon and Bath to Bristol, attaining a maximum speed of 79 mph at Lavington. From Bristol, LMS 2-6-2Ts Nos. 41202/3 took the train via Bristol Harbour, Yatton, the Wrington Light Railway, Yatton, Weston-Super-Mare, Highbridge, then running over the 'S&D' to Burnham before returning to Bristol, where 3440 was waiting with 2-6-2T No. 5528 to give assistance over the sharply graded North Somerset line through Radstock. No. 5528 came off at Westbury, No. 3440 returning to Paddington unassisted.

A very interesting tour was organised by publishers Ian Allan Ltd. on May 18 under the name 'The Daffodils Express'. *City of Truro* took over from No. 4090 *Dorchester Castle* at Gloucester and then ran via

With the small RCTS headboard on the top bracket, *City of Truro* passes St Anne's Park Bristol with the 'North Somerset Railtour' of April 28 1957. *W. Vaughan Jenkins.*

Hereford, Pontypool Road and the Vale of Neath line to Neath. As was WR practice, 2-6-0 No. 4358 was tucked inside as train engine for this stage of the journey, but as double-headed trains were not allowed over the since demolished Crumlin Viaduct, No. 3440 ran light across it, to be recoupled with the train on the other side. At Neath 2-6-2T No. 8104 was waiting to haul the train to Swansea to enable passengers to travel on the Mumbles Tramway. On the return journey Nos. 3440/4358 hauled the train from Swansea to

Newport, where its nine coach/284 tons load was taken on to Paddington by *Dorchester Castle* again.

On May 19 *City of Truro* made its first return run into Devonshire. This was a public excursion from Swindon to Kingswear with eight corridor coaches weighing 263 tons. Minimum speed on the west-bound run was 32 mph at Whiteball Summit. 2-6-2T No. 4179 assisted in both directions between Newton Abbot and Kingswear. The return non-stop 90.6 mile run from Teignmouth to Bristol was made in 101¾ minutes

A crowd of admirers gather on the platform at Bristol Temple Meads as No. 3440 *City of Truro* pauses in the sun with the RCTS 'North Somerset Railtour' of April 28 1957. *Gerald Siviour.*

Left: In beautiful late evening sun, *City of Truro* pilots 'Prairie' tank No. 5528 over Pensford viaduct, on the Bristol-Radstock-Frome branch, with the RCTS 'North Somerset Railtour' of April 28 1957.
Hugh Ballantyne.

Below: *City of Truro* and '4300' class Churchward 'Mogul' No. 4358 set a brisk pace en route from Gloucester to Hereford, with 'The Daffodils Express' of May 18 1957. a special organised by Ian Allan Ltd.
Tom Williams/National Railway Museum.

Lower: No. 3440 drifts away from Crumlin viaduct after uncoupling from 'The Daffodils Express' and running light across the steel structure, after which the train was brought across the valley by No. 4358. Double-headed trains were not permitted to cross this viaduct, since demolished.
R.J. Blenkinsop.

with 38 mph climbing to Whiteball Summit and a maximum speed of 83 mph at Wellington.

On June 16 *City of Truro* hauled the first of several SLS (Midland Area) tours to and from Swindon Works, with a seven-coach load. On the return run 80 mph was exceeded between Swindon and Didcot and again between Banbury and Leamington. On July 2 it was booked to work an educational excursion from Llanelly to Swindon but unfortunately its high cab roof struck the coal stage at Llanelly shed and some damage resulted to the roof and cab side. The next day it went to Caerphilly Works where the buckled cab roof and side-sheets were repaired and repainted, the engine running light to Swindon on July 5.

In August there came the news that the Caledonian Railway 4-2-2 No. 123 had entered St. Rollox Works for overhaul to work special trains, thereby following the precedent set by *City of Truro*. On August 18 the GWR 4-4-0 hauled the 11 coach/360 ton load of the RCTS 'Moonraker' from Paddington to Swindon and back. It was then noted that following its Caerphilly repair No. 3440 had acquired a modern short safety valve brass bonnet never carried by the engine in its previous working life. The following weekend it was the turn of the SLS again with a trip from Birmingham to Eastleigh Works, returning by the former MSWJ line to Swindon Works. On September 1 the SLS again arranged a trip from Birmingham to Swindon and back, with *City of Truro*, this time open to non-members. When next seen on a special train its tall safety valve bonnet had been restored. This was the Talyllyn Railway Preservation

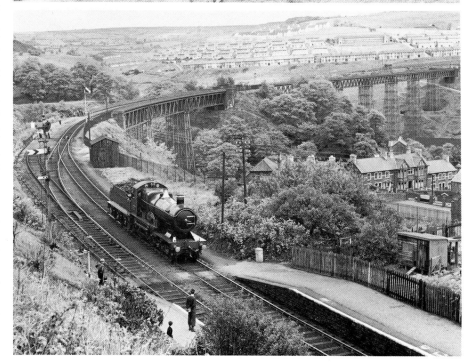

Above: On May 19 1957 *City of Truro* made its first public return to Devon, at the head of a Swindon–Kingswear excursion. The 4-4-0 is seen here taking the fast road through Dawlish Warren station. *L.F. Folkard.*

Left: A cab view of No. 3440 *City of Truro*. *R.J. Blenkinsop.*

City of Truro was still carrying out its regular weekday duties on the Didcot, Newbury & Southampton line. As far as specials were concerned *City of Truro*'s influence became reality in Scotland on March 18 1958 when Caledonian Railway 4-2-2 No. 123 ran in steam for the first time for 23 years on a train of two restored Caledonian coaches between Perth and Edinburgh. Unlike *City of Truro* though, CR No. 123 ran only on special occasions and was not regularly to be seen on scheduled passenger trains.

No. 3440's first 1958 sortie on a special train was on the Festiniog Railway Preservation Society train from Paddington to Ruabon and back on April 26 1958 with a load of eight coaches.

On May 11 it broke new ground by hauling a Ramblers' Special from Greenford to Horsted Keynes (now the northern terminus of the Bluebell Railway) as far as East Croydon. An immaculate Billinton 2-6-0, No. 32342, took the train on from there, while *City of Truro* went to Norwood Junction shed for servicing. Unfortunately, whilst running through the coal stage road to the turntable the cab roof made impact with the coal shute but fortunately without the serious consequences of the Llanelly mishap. The engine stood on shed all day among a number of types of LBSC engines before returning from East Croydon to Greenford in the evening.

By way of variety on Whit Sunday May 25 it hauled a photographic excursion from Exeter to Penzance and back sponsored by the 'Amateur Photographer' magazine with prizes given for the best photographs of the

Society special for their AGM at Towyn, worked between Paddington and Shrewsbury and back by *City of Truro* on September 28 1957.

Prior to that, though, on September 15 it made its first run into Cornwall, perhaps passing through Truro for the first time ever. It was

the 9.10 am excursion from Plymouth to Penzance with a load of 6 coaches weighing 185 tons. The engine worked down to Plymouth as pilot to the 5.30 am ex-Paddington service.

It must be remembered that as well as the glamour of special trains

Right: With its smokebox obscured by an appallingly unattractive headboard, *City of Truro* coasts into Bath Spa station from the east with an enthusiasts special on the sunny evening of June 15 1957. *Ivo Peters.*

Below: The erecting shop at Caerphilly Factory on July 5 1957, with *City of Truro* in residence for attention to the roof and left-hand cabside, damaged in an incident at Llanelly shed on July 2. The four men facing the camera are (left to right): Mr Stephens (Painter Chargeman), Mr George (Smiths Shop Foreman), Mr Davey (Erecting Shop Head Foreman) and Mr Carter (Erecting Shop Under Foreman). *Eric Mountford.*

Below right: *City of Truro* passes Small Heath and Sparkbrook station, Birmingham, with the return leg of an SLS special from Swindon on Sunday June 16 1957. *M. Mensing.*

day. Its six coaches were well patronised and with this load it required no assistance up the South Devon banks.

With the future of the DN&S Line somewhat insecure the engine's duties were changed in the 1958 summer service when it worked the 7.30 am Reading–Paddington semi-fast, returning on the 6.20 pm Paddington–Reading. Since these were business-men's trains *City of Truro* was much more in the public eye. The return duty involved tender first haulage of the 'Royal Duchy' empty stock from Old Oak Common carriage sidings up the Engine and Carriage Road, climbing the viaduct to cross the main line over to the down side. On a dry rail this presented no problems but on wet days and without the benefit of rear sanders it did cause difficulties and there were occasions when another engine hauled the empty stock and *City of Truro* ran light to Paddington.

Didcot men had enjoyed the visit of *City of Truro*. The engine, always kept spotless, brought them a new

August 18 1957: *City of Truro* awaits the rightaway at Paddington at 10.17 am with the RCTS 'Moonraker' special to Swindon. *Brian Morrison.*

Right: A day excursion from Swindon skirts the River Dart shortly after leaving Kingswear on May 19 1957 behind No. 3440 *City of Truro* and No. 4179, a '5100' class 2-6-2T. *L.F. Folkard.*

Below: With bicycle clips firmly in position to keep ash and dust at bay, *City of Truro*'s driver tops up the right-trailing axlebox oil reservoir at Swindon on August 18 1957, the day of the RCTS 'Moonraker' excursion.
Brian Morrison.

pride in the job and in their own words "it ran like a bird". In September 1958, with closure of the DN&S line only 18 months away, No. 3440 was transferred to Swindon. Circumstances were different to 1957 in that by 1958 the BRB had realised the profitability of special trains hauled by vintage engines, and preferred to utilise locomotives still in BR stock, often on unusual lines, so there was less demand for *City of Truro*'s service. However it was regularly used to haul Engineer's Inspection Saloons, and an even more important duty was rostered on September 10 when the locomotive hauled the Bristol Engineer's Saloon from Cardiff to Bristol with WR General Manager K.W.C. Grand on board in order to inspect the new Diesel Depot under construction at Marsh Junction. That having been done, the train continued to Swindon. With dieselisation gathering pace on the Western Region it became clear that *City of Truro*'s working days were numbered.

Its regular duty from Swindon was the working of the 5.32 pm Swindon to Bristol passenger, via Badminton, where it took over the Weston-super-Mare portion of the 5.6 pm semi-fast from Paddington, due at 9.21 pm, returning to Swindon as pilot engine to the 4.25 pm Plymouth–Swindon parcels train, leaving Weston at 10.25 pm. This was hauled by a 4-6-0 and usually loaded to between 20 and 30 bogie vans — a heavy train.

By April 1959 Scottish Region had followed suit with vintage steam in a big way. There was to be a Scottish Industries Fair at Kelvin Hall, Glasgow in the late summer and Highland Railway 'Jones Goods' 4-6-0 No. 103, stored for more than two decades as the Caley 'Single' had been, entered St Rollox Works for overhaul. In addition two engines were taken from traffic, North British Railway No. 256 *Glen Douglas* (BR No. 62469) to Cowlairs Works and Great North of Scotland Railway No. 49 *Gordon Highlander* (BR No. 62271) to Inverurie Works, both 4-4-0s.

The Fair was held from September 3–19, and the locomotives used to

haul the special trains were the four Scottish preserved engines together with *City of Truro*, which was thus breaking fresh ground once more. In general the trains were double-headed and *City of Truro* was the only preserved engine to haul a train on its own. The runs involving *City of Truro* were:

September 3 1959 GNS 49/3440 Montrose–Glasgow and return
September 5 1959 GNS 49/3440 Aberdeen–Glasgow and return
September 9 1959 3440 Aberdeen–Glasgow
September 16 1959 NBR 256/3440 Aberdeen–Glasgow and return
September 19 1959 NBR 256/3440 Aberdeen–Glasgow and return

On the September 9 outing No. 3440 was thought to be running slightly hot and a Stanier 4-6-0 was substituted for the return trip. In the event 3440 was not the only casualty as NBR No. 256 suffered a similar fault. By the year end No. 3440 was back at Swindon working occasional passenger trains to Bristol and back, being turned and serviced at Bath Road shed.

On March 18 1960 Class 9F 2-10-0 No. 92220 *Evening Star* was ceremonially named at Swindon Works as the last steam locomotive to be built by British Railways. Among other historic locomotives present and on display for the occasion were *City of Truro* and the Caledonian 'Single' 4-2-2 No. 123. These three engines were subsequently exhibited at Bristol Temple Meads, Taunton, Birmingham Moor Street and Paddington before No. 92220 worked its first special train for the Locomotive Club of Great Britain on April 3.

Top: The 12.42 pm Didcot–Newbury local makes good time near Upton & Blewbury with No. 3440 *City of Truro* in charge, in October 1957. The 12.42 from Didcot over the 'DN&S' was *City of Truro*'s regular duty in 1957. The round trip of 120 miles with approximately 100-ton trains called for little exertion by the 4-4-0 and long waits for 'time' at stations were a feature of the journey. *Dr J.A. Coiley.*

Above: *City of Truro* receives attention to its paintwork in the Swindon Works Erecting Shop on March 6 1960, in readiness for display at the naming ceremony of BR 9F 2-10-0 No. 92220 *Evening Star*. This ceremony was carried out by K.W.C. Grand on March 18 1960. *John C. Beckett.*

Left: With dock cranes and silos visible on the skyline, No. 3440 *City of Truro* awaits a clear road from Southampton Terminus with the 4.56 pm for Newbury on April 18 1957. *E.R. Morten.*

Left: *City of Truro* stands in gleaming splendour in 'A' shop at Swindon works, on March 18 1960. The 4-4-0 was displayed at the works to mark the occasion of the formal naming of 9F 2-10-0 No. 92220 *Evening Star*, carried out that day by K. W. C. Grand. *W. Potter.*

Below: With the blower on to raise steam, *City of Truro* awaits the guard's right-away to begin the next stage of its journey from Winchester Chesil station in May 1957, just a few weeks after emerging from York Railway Museum and a subsequent overhaul at Swindon. *S. C. Townroe.*

Above: The Westward TV exhibition train at Kensington (Olympia), with *City of Truro* on February 9 1961, before its West Country tour. *Mike Pope.*

Below: *City of Truro* and CR 4-2-2 No. 1 are hauled back to the stock shed at Swindon works following exhibition in 'A' shop during the naming ceremony for No. 92220 *Evening Star*. March 20 1960. *Ivo Peters.*

On April 20 *City of Truro* was partnered with the newly restored Midland 'Compound' 4-4-0 No. 1000, which had also been working special trains since restoration in September 1959. This trip was an Ian Allan special down the East Coast Main Line from Kings Cross to Doncaster Works, with an 11-coach load. Unfortunately No. 3440 ran hot on the return journey and had to be detached at Peterborough. The run was due to be repeated on April 26 but the last surviving B.12/3 4-6-0 No. 61572, now in course of restoration on the North Norfolk Railway, was substituted for the GWR engine. After this *City of Truro* was less frequently seen, having been in regular traffic for three years since its last general overhaul. However it worked the traditional SLS Special from Birmingham to and from Swindon Works on September 10 1960, this time also including visits to Southall and Reading sheds on the outward run.

On January 29 1961 it was being groomed at Swindon in readiness for a visit to Plymouth for the celebration of the opening of the Westward TV Studios. This was probably its last public appearance for it entered Swindon Works in April and was officially withdrawn from stock the following month. Although by now designated part of the National Collection, a new

Left: It's August 5 1957 and No. 3440 *City of Truro* leaves the 'DN&S' line at Shawford Junction with a Dicot–Southampton Terminus working. *Les Elsley.*

museum was being opened at Swindon, in view of the special significance of the GWR in the growth of that town. *City of Truro* entered the Museum in April 1962, where it was to be displayed with 'Star' Class 4-6-0 No. 4003 *Lode Star*, Dean Goods 0-6-0 No. 2516, Hawksworth 0-6-0PT No. 9400 and the broad gauge *North Star* replica built for the GWR Centenary celebrations in 1935. The Great Western Railway Museum at Swindon is housed in a building that has appropriate railway connections. Originally envisaged by Brunel as a lodging house for railway workers it soon became a Wesleyan Chapel, having last been used for this purpose in 1959. On June 24 1962 R.F. Hanks formally opened the Museum to the public.

In fact railway enthusiasts owe a great deal to the late R.F. Hanks for the privilege of seeing *City of Truro* at work or travelling behind it, as also to the late James Ness, former Scottish Region General Manager for following his example in bringing the 'Caley Single' out of retirement. *City of Truro* emerged once again from retirement in 1984 being hauled from Swindon to the Severn Valley Railway on July 13, for overhaul prior to service running as part of the celebrations in 1985 to mark the 150th anniversary of the incorporation of the GWR, on August 31 1835.

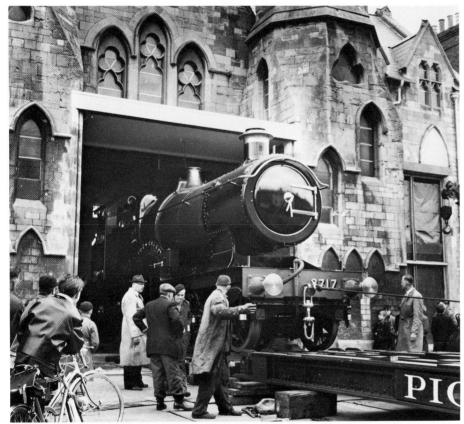

Top: With three coaches and a van on the tender drawbar, *City of Truro* leads a Southampton–Newbury train over Chapel Road Crossing, April 18 1957. *E.R. Morten.*

Centre: April 15 1962: *City of Truro* is winched slowly through the front wall of the GWR Museum, Faringdon Road, Swindon. The GWR Museum was a joint venture between Swindon Corporation, as it then was, and the British Railways Board. It is now operated by the Borough of Thamesdown with most of the exhibits, large and small, being on loan from the National Collection. *Mike Pope.*

Left: Into retirement for the second time, *City of Truro* stands in the GWR Museum flanked by Dean 'Goods' 0-6-0 No. 2516 and 'Star' 4-6-0 No. 4003 *Lode Star*. The Museum's origins as a Wesleyan Chapel are clearly apparent in this view.
National Railway Museum.

CHAPTER 5:

RENAISSANCE, 1985

by Alun Rees MA BSc

Chief Engineer, Severn Valley Railway

The Great Western Society's 1936-built 'Castle' 4-6-0 No. 5051 *Drysllwyn Castle* meets No. 3717 *City of Truro* at Bridgnorth, Severn Valley Railway on Monday September 10 1984. *City of Truro* had been displayed at Swindon Museum in its later GWR livery as No. 3717. *David Wilcock.*

CITY OF TRURO was resurrected from static display for the second time in its life on July 10 1984, when it was carefully winched through the dismantled front window of the GWR Museum, Faringdon Road Swindon, en-route for restoration at the Severn Valley Railway.

For the world at large, this was the first tangible sign of the 1903-built locomotive's 'second coming' — but for those involved behind the scenes, it was the culmination of one chapter of endeavour 'around the

table' and the start of another chapter of hard work actually restoring the locomotive to main line running order after 22 years in mothballs. The aim was of course to prepare the locomotive for a major part in 1985's celebrations to mark the 150th anniversary of the incorporation of the GWR.

The story had actually started a considerable time before this, as the National Railway Museum judged that the locomotive would make a considerable impact if it were to be

restored for steaming in 1985. At the end of 1983 at the invitation of Bill Bradshaw, then Western Region General Manager, I had attended a meeting at Paddington on October 13 1983. From this meeting emerged what was to become the 'GW150 Locomotive and Rolling Stock Committee', consisting of BR officers from the Mechanical & Electrical Engineers Departments and the Regional Operating Manager's Department, together with the Steam Locomotive Operators' Association,

BR Class 37 diesel-electric No. 37304 shunts *City of Truro* at Kidderminster on Saturday July 14 1984, in readiness for transfer to Severn Valley metals. *Hugh Ballantyne.*

National Railway Museum officers and representatives of some railway preservation bodies associated with the Great Western Railway. Steam running over BR lines in 1985 soon became a major item of discussion, together with the setting-up of a large static exhibition of GWR equipment at Swindon Works.

At this early stage, consideration was given to the possibility of the emergence of two of the GWR's most historic engines, *City of Truro* and *Lode Star* from their resting place, the GWR Museum, at Swindon, and the committee resolved that preliminary examination should be made of both locomotives to establish the feasibility of restoring one or both to working order.

At the request of the NRM, and by courtesy of the Museum authorities at Swindon a joint examination of both engines by BR and SVR engineers was carried out within the limited confines of the Swindon museum and this revealed firstly that No. 4003 *Lode Star* (built 1907) had two tyres worn below scrapping size and a very poor firebox! This ruled out any reasonable chance of restoration to running condition. However, *City of Truro* did not appear to be too bad a proposition after a first exam, the most suspect item being the tender.

Unfortunately, the firebox had been painted white on the inside for exhibition purposes, and this prevented any close examination of the copper plates and stay-heads. Some of the steel stays obviously required changing, due to wasting on the water side, but all in all, the locomotive appeared to be a reasonable proposition for restoration to working order.

At the next meeting of the Locomotive and Rolling Stock group on December 14 1983, the condition of the two locomotives was discussed and the SVR put a proposal jointly to the NRM, as the authority responsible for *City of Truro*, and to BR, that an attempt should be made to restore the engine to main line running condition for the celebrations in 1985, if it could be removed from the museum and taken to the SVR works at Bridgnorth.

I shall not dwell in detail on the long chain of events which led up to the actual removal of the engine from the museum in July 1984, but I should hate readers to underestimate the huge number of problems this presented. Suffice to say that the Science Museum, the National Railway Museum, Thamesdown Borough Council, the staff of the GWR Museum and British Rail were all very heavily involved in making the extremely complex and detailed arrangements necessary. The removal of the frontage of the Museum, the closure of Faringdon Road (Swindon's main street) whilst the engine and tender were loaded onto road vehicles and road haulage into the Works were only three of the hundreds of problems that had to be overcome.

Overcome they were, however,

A view of *City of Truro*'s boiler whilst undergoing repair at the SVR's Bridgnorth works. *Ian McDonald.*

Above: *City of Truro* stands in Bridgnorth yard in BR lined black — a livery it never carried at any time — on Wednesday November 7 1984. This was done in connection with an 'April Fool' spoof published in the April issue of 'Steam Railway' magazine. *Peter J.C. Skelton.*

Left: The locomotive frames during repair in the SVR workshop, March 1985. *Ian McDonald.*

Below left: A view inside the smokebox during boiler repairs. Compare this view with the picture on page 8. *Ian McDonald.*

Below right: SVR boilersmith Graham Beddow reams out defective stays in the firebox tubeplate. *Ian McDonald.*

and eventually a team of BR engineers, under the direction of Jock Smith, dismantled the inside motion, uncoupled the engine and tender and supervised their loading onto road vehicles. The loading and transport to the Works had to be undertaken at night to avoid too much disruption to road traffic. Engine and tender were rapidly re-railed and reunited in the Civil Engineers' Stores at the works and were soon hustled away under lock and key.

Movement to Kidderminster by rail via Gloucester and Worcester took place overnight on July 13 and *City of Truro* was handed over to the care of GWR 0-6-0 No. 3205 for haulage to Bridgnorth on the morning of July 14.

The first plan was to keep the engine intact until the SVR Enthusiasts Weekend in September although some exploratory work was to be carried out in the meantime. A joint inspection of the boiler by SVR, BR(LMR) and BR(WR) boiler inspectors led to the suggestion of

a very gentle attempt at steam raising to ascertain the possibility of leaks in the firebox and also as a means of testing the fittings and boiler mountings. However, this idea was stillborn, as the first attempt at filling the boiler with water revealed large numbers of burst tubes. Back to square one! The

first attempt at filling the tender proved equally disastrous with water pouring out, seemingly everywhere. So much for a sneaky try-out!

The engine thus lay dormant until after the Enthusiasts' Weekend during which it was posed in the shed yard at Bridgnorth where it soon became a focal point for visitors.

In early October a start was finally made in stripping the engine. However, before anything was removed from the outside, the 'April Fool' joke of painting *City of Truro* in BR lined black livery was conceived. 'Nula Seer', a gentleman who looks very like me when viewed in a mirror, perpetrated this 'vandalism' in close collaboration with the editor of a certain railway monthly devoted to steam railway matters! SVR Paintshop Foreman Andy Williams and his team carried out a remarkably quick paint job complete with full mixed-traffic lining (one side only) in only two days. Twelve hours — and several feet of film — later *City of Truro* was green again and no-one would ever have guessed! Now that the dust has settled, I would only comment that anyone who saw *City of Truro* in lined black and could look at the engine dispassionately could not but agree that it looked absolutely beautiful — but that's another story!

Dismantling gathered pace thereafter, with the aim of removing the boiler from the frames for a full examination: the boiler tubes were removed, the cab loosened, saddle bolts removed, and so on. It was at this stage that the whole schedule for repair was thrown into total chaos, really before it got properly under way. SVR-based 4-6-0 No. 7819 *Hinton Manor* was also undergoing a general repair at Bridgnorth, hopefully concurrently with the 'City', the 4-6-0 being required to work the inaugural Bristol–Plymouth train with No. 6000 *King George V* in July 1985. However, due to the West of England resignalling scheme and numerous other engineering works, the date for the inaugural train was brought forward to April 7, thus bringing the required completion date for *Hinton Manor* forward by a full three months! Work on the 'City' therefore had to wait until the 'Manor's' boiler was completed in late January!

City of Truro's boiler was removed in the middle of a bitter freeze-up in January and a further conference of boiler inspectors was held, to finally ascertain the repair requirement now that full access was available. Removal of the white paint in the firebox enabled a full inspection of the platework to be made for the first time. The result was not too good — paint can hide a multitude of ills. The net result was a formidable 'shopping list' of repairs:—

Weld in new flanges on both sides of the copper door-plate and fit 50 copper studs.
Reinforce flanges in copper tube-plate.
Renew all steel rivets in tube-plate.
Renew 700 stays.
Renew all 14 superheater elements.
Renew all 276 boiler tubes and 14 superheater flues.

Additionally, whilst the above repairs were being carried out, two further extensive cracks were discovered in the copper door-plate and two more in the back corners of the foundation ring. These were all grooved-out and welded.

Concurrently with this boiler work a start was made on the mechanical repairs. Closer examination of the tender-bottom revealed that the well was completely rotten and most of the seam rivets had no heads. It was deemed quicker and easier to replace the whole of the bottom and so the tank was removed from the frames, turned upside-down and the old well was cut out. New platework was fabricated and then welded into place and the tank returned to the frames. Whilst the tank was off the frames, the opportunity was taken to renew the front framing on each side as this was badly wasted. Lastly, the footplate of the tender was rebuilt completely in steel, as this had been made of wood for museum exhibition.

With the tender and boiler repairs in progress, the mechanical parts of the engine were examined before reassembly of the motion. The valves and pistons were removed for examination of the bores and rings: the cylinders and steam-chest liners were found to be in good condition but the piston rings required renewing. The whole of the motion was in good condition however, with very little attention required beyond reassembly.

The three steam brake cylinders on engine and tender were all found to be seized and these were removed and overhauled. Examination of the injectors came next and this revealed a major crisis, for on stripping the exhaust injector, the cupboard was found to be bare — the 'cones', essential internal parts, were missing. This was a major setback as the injector would not work without them and no spares were available on the SVR. An urgent phone call to Swindon got a BR Mechanical Inspector examining the exhaust injector on *Lode Star*. Guess what? No cones!! On the assumption that Swindon removed these items when preparing engines for museum exhibition, it seemed probable that the Science Museum's No. 4073 *Caerphilly Castle* would not have any either. To the best of my knowledge, the final possible source of spares was the NRM's 28xx 2-8-0 No. 2818, which had been overhauled at Eastleigh. A telephone call to John Bellwood's staff at York revealed that 2818's exhaust injector appeared to be complete. A quick exchange was arranged and on arrival at Bridgnorth an examination revealed it to be intact. However, closer examination showed the body casting to be extensively cracked — presumably old frost damage. This was repaired with the hope that the cure would prove complete under steam. All the cab fittings and boiler mountings were checked, overhauled and made ready for replacement.

After the 'Nula Seer' incident, it was obvious that the finished livery of the locomotive would be a major topic of discussion. As the locomotive is not in its 'as built' condition, it would not be historically correct to paint it in the livery it originally carried. To overcome this problem of historical accuracy and to meet what was apparently a popular demand for a different and dramatic GWR livery, the NRM suggested the adoption of the special 'celebration' livery introduced on a few of the major express locomotives in 1897 to celebrate the Diamond Jubilee of Queen Victoria. As built the 'City' was not superheated, did not have top-feed water delivery and was fitted with slide valves — in its present condition the plain green livery with black underframes, as displayed at the GWR Museum at Swindon, was correct.

However, in order the achieve the 1903 colour scheme, the SVR paintshop staff have extensively researched the original paintwork actually applied to the engine and tender by carefully examining the bottom layers of between 15 and 20 coats of paint. These colours have been very carefully matched and so we can say, without contradiction, that the colours applied to the finished locomotive in 1985 were as near as humanly possible to those applied in 1903. Any complaints, therefore, should be directed towards the 1903 paintshop foreman at Swindon Works!

After arrival from the GWR Museum, Swindon, and before stripping for restoration began, No. 3717 *City of Truro* shares the shed yard at Bridgnorth, Severn Valley Railway, with 'Hall' 4-6-0 No. 6960 *Raveningham Hall*. Restoration of the 4-4-0 to working order has involved the re-adoption of the original number 3440 and the elaborate Edwardian livery as depicted on the front cover. *Nigel Harris.*

CONCLUSION

M.J. Draper

General Manager, Severn Valley Railway

THE Severn Valley Railway has been the proud host of many important events, people and engines in it's 20-year history. None have compared, however, with the pride we felt when we were selected and entrusted with the restoration of what can only be described as one of the most famous and historic steam engines of this new steam age.

City of Truro is a magnificent machine, an absolute jewel of Edwardian engineering practice, and as pleasing to the eye as any locomotive to ride the iron road. To be involved so deeply with this momentous restoration project has been a source of the greatest inspiration to both paid staff and volunteers alike at Bridgnorth who gave so selflessly to the project. It is a due reward also for everyone who gave so generously to the restoration fund operated by SLOA, a fund that of course remains open to those who have yet to support it, and which will no doubt receive a most welcome boost from the proceeds of this book.

No mention of *City of Truro* would be complete without also paying tribute to the staffs of the National Railway Museum, York, the Science Museum, London, Thamesdown Borough Council, and the GWR Museum, Swindon, who between them took the brave decision to release the engine for the enjoyment of an even greater audience, and on the main line as well!

We have all derived a great sense of satisfaction from returning this engine to steam. We will no doubt derive yet more actually using it, and we look forward to welcoming everyone with an eye for locomotive beauty to 'the Valley' whilst *City of Truro* is our honoured guest.

Michael Draper.

APPENDIX 1

CITY of Truro's sprint down Wellington bank on May 9 1904 received comprehensive coverage in the pages of 'The Railway Magazine' which at the time of the record-breaking run was barely seven years old.

Charles Rous-Marten's account of the up 'Ocean Mail' special of May 9 1904 was published in the June 1904 issue of 'The Railway Magazine', under the headline 'Railway Speed: The Great Western Railway's Record of Records'. Rous-Marten was a recognised authority on steam locomotive performance, and his report of the run also appeared in 'The Engineer' of May 20 1904. However, it is amazing to note that the actual maximum speed achieved during the descent of Wellington bank, according to his observations, is not mentioned anywhere in his 'Railway Magazine' article — at the request of the GWR. Although he was acutely aware of the locomotive's achievement, he had to be content with the allusion to the "hurricane descent" of the bank. It is of interest to note that it was the June issue of the 'Railway Magazine' — published on June 1 — which carried Rous-Marten's report of this run, which had occurred just 23 days previously. Editor G.A. Sekon would probably not normally be gathering editorial material so close to the journal's publication date, and the appearance of this article so soon after the run is a measure of its importance, and seems to indicate some last-minute rearrangement of the June issue's contents. The article was squeezed into a plain double-page spread, without illustrations, and appeared in addition to the June instalment of Rous-Marten's monthly 'British Locomotive Practice and Performance' column.

RAILWAY SPEED: THE GREAT WESTERN RAILWAY'S RECORD OF RECORDS
(Railway Magazine; June 1904, pp. 502/3)

RECORDS crowd upon records in this remarkable year of railway history. But the Great Western Railway's latest feat really does look like something of a climax which may be expected to remain unassailed for a long time to come. Indeed under existing conditions it could not easily be beaten, except by the removal of the three adverse conditions of Monday May 9th, viz., the permanent way slow near Starcross, the accidental check at Wellington, and the severe slacking over the Cricklade Bridge under repairs. These certainly represented an aggregate abnormal hindrance of 5 minutes. The normal hindrances, viz., the slowings through Exeter and Bath and around the Bristol avoiding line, must, I fear, be deemed virtually permanent. The present Great Western Railway speed record has its solid practical side in the fact that it was attempted and achieved for purely business reasons of wide importance. And its success meant that the mails from America and also from Australia and New Zealand, via San Francisco, as well as the bullion representing the American payment to France on account of the price of the Panama Canal, all reached London from New York in the shortest transit time ever effected, viz., 5 days 21 hours 58 minutes, including all delays by land and sea. That is a record of which everybody concerned may reasonably be proud.

The North German Lloyd steamer **Kronprinz Wilhelm** left New York on May 3rd, at 3.10 p.m., and reached Plymouth Sound on May 9th, at 8 a.m. It was a perfect morning, clear and bright, and the Devonian and Cornish scenery was a veritable dream of verdant beauty. But we had little time to admire after the big steamer had dropped anchor. She had made the Atlantic crossing in 5 days, 21 hours, averaging 22.6 knots, or 26 miles an hour. Our function now was to get her very heavy mails up to Bristol and London with all possible celerity. The transfer of some 1,300 big bags was effected with admirable smartness, the bags being sorted as they were put into the tender, those for Bristol, Wales and the Midlands, and the North being kept separate, so that when we reached the Millbay pier they could at once be loaded into the rear van, which was to be dropped outside Bristol. At 9.19 a.m. our "Ocean Mail Special" was ready, and it was duly taken to the main line at Millbay Dock Crossing whence we were to take our formal departure.

The train comprised five heavily laden double-bogie eight-wheeled postal vans, one being still a larger sorting van; the total weight, including mails and specie, was estimated at 148 tons exclusive of engine and tender. Our engine was No. 3440 "City of Truro", one of Mr Churchward's fine "City" class, with 6 foot 8 inch four-coupled wheels, inside cylinders 18 by 26 inches, extended wagon-top boiler and Belpaire firebox. The driver was Clements, a very smart man, who has given me some capital runs with "Herschel" of the "Atbara" type. We made our definite start at 9.23.10 a.m. It took us 3 minutes 7 seconds to clear North Road, 70 chains, and then we begin to "go". The terrific climb from Plympton to Hemerdon, 2¼ miles out of the 3¼ being on a continuous rise at 1 in 41, was accomplished in 3 minutes 55 seconds, and Wrangaton summit was breasted in 16 minutes 41 seconds from Plymouth North Road, a climb of 14 miles 10 chains, while the later ascent for 4 miles 65 chains from Totnes to Dainton, some being at 1 in 40, occupied only 5 minutes 1 second. Then came the service slack past Newton Abbot, the easing for the Teignmouth curves, the severe slowing for the 1½-mile of single line through the five tunnels near Dawlish, a still worse slackening for permanent way works near Starcross, and a dead slow to walking pace in Exeter station. Yet we passed Exeter in 59 minutes 2 seconds from the Millbay start, and 55 minutes 55 seconds from Plymouth North Road, the latter being a distance of 52 miles 3 chains over the hardest road in the kingdom.

Then came the climb of 20 miles to Whiteball Summit, the last 2½ miles at 1 in 115, up which our speed never fell below 62 miles an hour followed by a "hurricane descent" of the Wellington bank, nearly spoiled, however, by a check from some foolish platelayers calmly staying on the "four foot" when the "lightning special" was close on them; and a steady persistence of high even speed along the level length which virtually extends from Taunton to Bristol. We stopped at Pylle Hill Junction on the avoiding line, having made the run of 75¼ miles from Exeter in the astonishing time of 64 minutes 17 seconds, and having covered the 128½ miles from Millbay in 123 minutes 9 seconds, while our time for the 128 miles from Plymouth North Road was 120 minutes 12 seconds. At Pylle Hill Junction we cut off the Bristol mail van and also changed engines, it being doubtful whether our coal

would carry us on to London at such speed as was contemplated. So No. 3065 "Duke of Connaught" a 7 foot 8 inch single, with leading bogie, driver Underhill, came on and we started again, after a stay of 3 minutes 43 seconds, with a load of four eight-wheelers, or about 120 tons behind the tender. What with the long slow round Bristol by the avoiding line — we took 3 minutes 39 seconds to clear Bristol East Box — and the service slow to 10 miles an hour through Bath station, we spent 39 minutes 37 seconds on the 41¼ miles to Swindon. We slackened badly through the station so as to be able to cross the Cricklade Bridge — undergoing heavy repairs — at walking pace, but then we blazed forth in full glory, experiencing no further hindrances save the slight one of picking up water near Goring, until we arrived at Paddington, after a run of 3 hours 46 minutes 48 seconds from Millbay Dock Crossing to the final stop; 3 hours 46 minutes 28 seconds to the spot inside of Paddington station where we had stopped two days previously — ie 223 minutes 21 seconds — from Plymouth North Road to Paddington. The run from Bristol, 118½ miles, was done in 99 minutes 18 seconds to the Paddington platform, 99 minutes 26 seconds to the inside of the station, 99 minutes 46 seconds to the stop. From Bath, passing dead slow, we came to London in 85 minutes 40 seconds, platform to platform. But the Swindon–London run was the climax. Notwithstanding the slack almost to a walking pace at Cricklade Bridge, which cost us more than a minute, we actually ran Swindon platform to Paddington platform in 59 minutes 41 seconds — 19 seconds under the hour for 77¼ miles. From Didcot into Paddington station we took 40 minutes 18 seconds, from Reading 27 minutes 17 seconds, from Slough 14 minutes 23 seconds. Also we ran from Reading to Slough, 17½ miles, in 12 minutes 54 seconds, and from Wootton Bassett to Westbourne Park, 81¾ miles, in 62 minutes 55 seconds. Such figures simply make one gasp.

The following is the condensed log of this wonderful run:

Millbay Dock Crossing	dep.	9.23.10
Plymouth (North Road)	pass.	9.26.17
Newton Abbot	pass.	9.59.52
Exeter	pass.	10.22.12
Whiteball Summit	pass.	10.41.41
Taunton	pass.	10.50.01
Bristol (Pylle Hill)	arr.	11.26.29
	dep.	11.30.12
Bath	pass.	11.43.50
Chippenham	pass.	11.56.00
Swindon	pass.	12.09.49
Didcot	pass.	12.29.20
Reading	pass.	12.42.21
Slough	pass.	12.55.15
Paddington, platform end	arr.	1.09.30
Paddington, in station	arr.	1.09.38
Paddington, final stop	arr.	1.09.58

I may add that I travelled at the courteous invitation of the Superintendent of the Line whose assistant superintendent, Mr Aldington, took able charge throughout, and Inspector Llewellyn efficiently superintended operations on the footplate. The respective drivers, Clements and Underhill, handled their fine engines splendidly. The road was kept absolutely clear from first to last and the travelling was perfect in its smoothness and steadiness.

CHARLES ROUS MARTEN.

The GWR was firmly convinced that official recognition and publication of Rous-Marten's figures and maximum speed would frighten passengers away from its trains and continued it's policy of keeping City of Truro's

exploit quiet. Rous-Marten wrote to GWR General Manager James Inglis, recommending that the events of May 9 1904 should be made public, but this was not taken up. (See Appendix 2) Consequently, in the June 1906 instalment of 'British Locomotive Practice and Performance' Rous-Marten was once again only able to allude to City of Truro's run down Wellington bank, just over a year earlier.

BRITISH LOCOMOTIVE PRACTICE & PERFORMANCE,
(Railway Magazine, June 1906, p. 462).

. . . The absolute maximum speed that I have ever recorded upon railway on earth was reached in a special trial which I prefer not to indicate more specifically than by saying that the engine was four-coupled and had 6ft. 8in. driving wheels. On this occasion a series of quarter miles occupied the following times: 10 secs., 9.8 secs., 9.4 secs., 9.2 secs., 8.8 secs.; the last, of course, representing a rate of 102.3 miles an hour. It will be observed that the fastest half-mile was covered in exactly 18 secs., or at the rate of just 100 miles an hour, and that the speed for the whole mile, taken in successive quarters, and also as a whole, was 96.8. The locality was on a somewhat sharply falling gradient, but the road was one of the best in England, and the performance was not attended by the slightest amount of danger, while the travelling was as smooth as any I have ever experienced. I feel sure that these figures, which I have not previously published in England, will be read with much interest.

By 1922, the editorial chair of 'British Locomotive Practice and Performance' had been taken over by Cecil J. Allen, and in the July issue of 'The Railway Magazine' for that year, City of Truro's 'Ocean Mail' run of May 9 1904 was once more under analysis. The reason for 'CJ's' re-examination of the run was to mark the completion of 25 years of locomotive practice articles within the pages of 'The Railway Magazine', which had been established in 1897.

BRITISH LOCOMOTIVE PRACTICE & PERFORMANCE
(Railway Magazine, July 1922, p. 41)

Now comes the colossal feat of May 9 1904, when Mr Rous-Marten, a traveller by the racing train, was privileged to record the astounding time of 3 hours 46 min 48 sec from the start at Millbay Crossing — a good two minutes further off in time than North Road — via Pylle Hill Junction at Bristol, where a stop of 3 min 43 sec was made, and the Bristol avoiding line to Paddington, a distance of precisely 246½ miles.

. . . Though somewhat faster than customary, the downhill speeds were restrained to Newton, where speed was reduced, following which came the single line reductions at Teignmouth and Dawlish, and a bad permanent way slowing at Starcross. After the Exeter slack, fine work was done up to Whiteball, the distance of 20 miles, all but 5 chains, taking 19 min 29 sec only. The minimum speed claimed by Rous-Marten on the 1 in 115 at the summit — 62mph — is however clearly an error, as the average from Burlescombe to Whiteball was only 54.4; presumbly 52mph was the figure meant. On the Wellington side of the bank Mr Rous-Marten claimed that maximum of 102.3mph was reached, the average speed for ½-mile being 100, and for a full mile 96mph, between Wellington and Norton Fitzwarren — a feat which was all but spoiled by the persistence of certain platelayers in staying calmly on the 'four-foot' until the special was nearly on them.

C.J. Allen's opinion of Rous-Marten was a high one; nevertheless he had pinpointed what he believed to be an error in his predecessor's recording of *City of Truro* (the 62mph speed noted at Whiteball summit) and whilst he did not challenge the 102.3mph speed claim for the descent of Wellington bank, the seeds of doubt were sown.

From the GWR's point of view, here was an enthusiast's railway journal discussing in detail an event which officially it had failed even to acknowledge as having happened. This was rectified in the November issue of the GWR's own magazine, as reported in the December 1922 issue of 'The Railway Magazine' under the simple headline '102 MPH'.

PERTINENT PARAGRAPHS
(Railway Magazine, December 1922, p. 467)

In the November number of our Great Western contemporary particulars are included of a report made by the late Mr Charles Rous-Marten to the then General Manager of the Great Western Railway, Mr (after Sir) James Inglis, in regard to the famous run with an Ocean Mail special from Plymouth, when a speed of 102.3mph was claimed for 4-4-0 engine No. 3440 City of Truro. In general the particulars now issued under official sanction will be common knowledge to readers of the RAILWAY MAGAZINE. In fact, in the June 1904 number the first published after the run was made, a complete log, as now published, was included in a special article by the late Mr Charles Rous-Marten. No mention was, however, made of the fact that so high a maximum speed was reached, but in the June 1906 number the quarter-mile times were given by Mr Rous-Marten in his ordinary article, though only by inference could it be associated with the particular run. It has, however, been general knowledge for many years past that this speed was attained on this run, and in several editions of the Railway Year Book a paragraph to that effect has been included in the "Railway Miscellany", after having been given as a reply in 'The Why and the Wherefore' section of The Railway Magazine. Further, in the July 1922 number of The Railway Magazine Mr Cecil J. Allen discussed the run, comparing the times in detail with other notable examples of Great Western locomotive performance, incidentally pointing out an error made by Mr Rous-Marten. Although our Great Western contemporary is hardly correct in suggesting that their publication is a "revelation" it is of interest in that Mr Rous-Marten's "confidential" report to the General Manager is now made public under official auspices.

AS described in Chapter 2, by Keith M. Beck, *City of Truro* was withdrawn from service and presented to The Railway Museum, York, in recognition of its record-breaking run of May 9 1904. However, in the July 1934 issue of 'The Railway Magazine', Cecil J. Allen really 'set the cat among the pigeons' in his 'British Locomotive Practice and Performance' column by disputing that 102.3 mph had been achieved by *City of Truro*. As might be expected, this prompted substantial correspondence and the events of May 9 1904 were dealt with exensively by 'CJ' in his column in the July, September, October and December issues for that year.

Extracts from 'The Railway Magazine' 1904–1922 reproduced courtesy of John Slater, Editor 'The Railway Magazine'.

APPENDIX 2

AS NOTED in Appendix 1, Rous-Marten's wishes were that the GWR should not suppress details of 'City of Truro's' run down Wellington bank on May 9 1904. Just over a year after this run, Rous-Marten wrote to GWR General Manager James (later Sir James) Inglis, with his reasoning for full disclosure Rous Marten died in 1908, his wishes unfulfilled.

Eldon Chambers
30 Fleet Street
London E.C.

PRIVATE   June 20 1905
James C. Inglis Esqr.
Dear Mr. Inglis,

Pursuant to my recent letter and in accordance with the suggestion in your letter of 7th inst., I now "take up the correspondence at the point at which it ceased" relative to the question of publishing the maximum speed in your Record Run of May 1904.

First, let me state my own side of the case: The Great Western is wooing public favour and, very properly, seeking to increase traffic to the Far West by means of extra-fast non-stopping trains.

Now, I happened last year to hear a good deal of conversation with reference in particular to those Paddington–Plymouth non-stop runs. To my surprise, many people of different ages, sexes and callings, declared that nothing would induce them to travel by trains which ran at such "fearful speeds". Whenever opportunity decently offered, I "cut in" and pointed out that in reality these trains did not run, or need to run, nearly so fast as many other Great Western trains which had been running unnoticed for a number of years, and that the time was gained, not through extra speeds, but through lighter loads and absence of stops. This was received with a good deal of incredulity, but when I proved my case, first by the actual figures and secondly by the proof (although of course without giving the actual maximum) that with the Ocean Specials I had on more than one occasion recorded speeds enormously higher than the fastest that are run by the trains in question, and that at those times the travelling with the smoothest, easiest and therefore safest of any, I was able to compel conviction.

Now this is the basis of my proposal that the maximum attained by those non-passenger-carrying Specials which was from 30 to 50% higher than that run by those best regular long-distance Expresses, should now be made public 'pour encourager les autres', or at any rate, to make the travelling public see that when going by your best regular trains, they will not run at a rate at all approaching that which has been attained with perfect ease and safety by non-passenger or experimental Specials.

You have doubtless noticed letters in the papers referring to "terrific" or "dangerous" speed being run by regular expresses such as "70 to 80 miles an hour". But the Record Mail Special **averaged** 70.2 from the Exeter slow pass to the Bristol stop, and 71.5 from the Bristol start to the Paddington stop, notwithstanding the delays of the Bath Service-slack and the very bad special slow over the Cricklade Bridge under repair, while, between Swindon and Paddington, we maintained a steady average of **80** miles an hour for **73 miles on end**.

These facts have of course been published already; indeed could be readily gathered from the published log of the train. The actual maximum rate has not, so far, got into print. Indeed, I am not aware that anybody but myself recorded it with absolute accuracy, although I suspect that one of the Post Office people must have done some timing for he came very near the truth in that Plymouth paper's article which I sent you, and which gives an illustration of "City of Truro" averaging 99 to 100 miles an hour. But of course a mere statement in a daily newspaper carries but little weight.

CONFIDENTIAL

In now giving you my actual figures, it is I feel sure, unnecessary for me to stipulate that they shall be regarded as strictly confidential, and that in no case shall my information be used to anybody's prejudice. Upon that I am quite certain I can depend without any specific pledge on your part.

What happened then was this: When we topped the Whitehall Summit, we were still doing 63 miles an hour; when we emerged from the Whiteball tunnel we had reached 80; thenceforward our velocity rapidly and steadily increased, the quarter-mile times diminishing from 11 seconds at the tunnel entrance to 10.6 seconds, 10.2 seconds, 10.0 sec., 9.8 sec., 9.2 sec., and finally to 8.8 sec., this last being equivalent to a rate of 102.3 miles an hour. The two quickest quarters thus occupied exactly 18 seconds for the half-mile, equal to 100 miles an hour. All this time the travelling was so curiously smooth that but for the sound it was difficult to believe we were moving at all, and the perfect control retained over the train was strikingly manifested through what apeared at the time the vexatious incident of those platelayers dawdling on the 4-foot way, which compelled a sudden reduction of the speed by about one-half, which was effected in the readiest and simplest way conceivable, without the slightest jerk or irregularity.

And now "the murder is out". It seems to me to afford a strong argument for the consolation of the timid folk who might otherwise be deterred from enjoying the comfort and celerity of your splendid express, to be able to impress upon them that at the highest speed they would travel, they would be going quite slowly compared with that at which the Mail-special ran with entire ease and safety. I hope you will agree with me in this opinion.

I imagine this is the information that you desired to receive; anything more that you wish to learn on the subject, I shall have much pleasure in communicating, and if you can spare me a few minutes in the early part of next week, I shall be duly appreciative.

With kind regards
I remain
Yours very truly
CHARLES ROUS-MARTEN

IN Chapter 3 Keith M. Beck described the events leading to No. 3717 *City of Truro*'s arrival at the old York Railway Museum, and quoted selectively from the correspondence between the Museum, and officers of the Great Western and London and North Eastern Railways. The correspondence is printed here in full, courtesy of the National Railway Museum, York.

The first letter in the sequence was from E.M. Bywell, Secretary and Curator of the Railway Museum, York, to Robert Bell, the LNER Assistant General Manager at Kings Cross.

York,
6th August 1930.

Dear Mr Bell,
THE RAILWAY MUSEUM, YORK.
Offer of famous engine.
I saw Mr Boyd-Carpenter at Doncaster yesterday. Apparently he is a friend of Mr Collett, Chief Mechanical Engineer of the Great Western Railway. His story is that Mr Collett has told him that if he can find a permanent home for the "City of Truro" engine, which is shortly to be out of traffic, he is at liberty to do so.
I think the real position is that we are being sounded in this round-about way as to whether we would accept the engine if offered and I am asked by Mr Boyd-Carpenter that nothing about this tentative offer should be allowed to leak out.
"The City of Truro" is really one of the most famous engines in the world, having, in May 1904, made a world's speed record of 102.3 miles per hour on a journey on an American special mail train. The story of this feat is recorded in all good books on railways and the latest to be issued mentions that the record still stands unbeaten.
I feel sure that this engine would be a great acquisition to our Museum and make it more than ever regarded as a national railway Valhalla. It was hinted to me that, should the engine come to the Museum, its last journey would be made in a blaze of publicity and that it should first be exhibited for charity, just as was the "Gladstone" (LB&SC engine) before it came to York. Troops of people come especially from different places to see the "Gladstone" and "the City of Truro" would bring more visitors still.
Mr Rudgard says that he might be able to squeeze another locomotive into the Museum, but I am getting him the exact dimensions of "the City of Truro". I think it well, however, to write you this preliminary letter so that in the event of your having any definite views against the acceptance of the engine from the Great Western Company, you can let me know so that I may stop negotiations: otherwise if Mr Rudgard's report is favourable I will arrange a Museum Committee meeting and send forward to you their recommendations.
Mr Hornsby is away from the office so that I have not been able to make him aware of the offer, but he is a firm upholder

APPENDIX 3

of the Museum and I feel sure he would be in favour of acceptance, if the cost of getting the engine to the Museum is not going to be prohibitive.
Yours faithfully,
E.M. Bywell, Secretary & Curator of the Railway Museum.

Almost six weeks later, Bywell sent a memo to Mr H.J. Rudgard:

H.J. Rudgard Esq.   16th September 1930
THE RAILWAY MUSEUM, YORK.
The "City of Truro"
I attach a further letter I have received from Mr Boyd-Carpenter. I think that if the engine is accepted for the Museum we should certainly have along with it a tender of the original type. However, on hearing from you that you are able to get the locomotive into the Museum, I propose to call a meeting of the Museum Committee.
E.M. Bywell, Secretary & Curator of the Railway Museum.
(NB: the letter from Mr Boyd-Carpenter mentioned by Bywell is not included here).

Rudgard clearly supported Bywell's enthusiasm for adding *City of Truro* to the Museum and replied to the memo the following day:

E.M. Bywell Esq.,   17th September 1930
The Railway Museum, York.
In reply to yours of the 15th and 16th and the enclosed papers I herewith enclose you Drawing 30 EP 214 showing a re-arrangement of the exhibits in the Queen Street shed to enable the "City of Truro" to be added to the collection. You will note that the "City of Truro" is shown in red and the re-arranged exhibits in green.
H.J. Rudgard.

As promised, Bywell called a meeting of the Museum Committee, which met for the 22nd time on September 22 1930. Minute 163 recorded:

Mr Boyd-Carpenter, Doncaster, explained to the Committee that the Great Western engine "The City of Truro" would shortly be taken out of traffic. This engine is credited with having made the world's speed record (102.3 miles per hour) in May 1904 when drawing the Ocean Mail Special from Plymouth to Paddington. For 73 miles on end the train is said to have run at 80 miles an hour. The entire distance (243 miles) was accomplished in 3 hours 46 minutes 48 seconds, an average speed, start to stop and including checks and stops, of 65.49 miles per hour. Mr Boyd-Carpenter explained that he is acquainted with Mr Collett, the Chief Mechanical Engineer of the Great Western Company, who is anxious that such a note-worthy engine should not be scrapped.
It has been decided that the most suitable resting place would be the Railway Museum, York and Mr Boyd-Carpenter

intimated that he was authorised by Mr Collett on behalf of the Great Western Company to offer the engine to the Museum. After discussion it was agreed, on the proposition of Mr Hornsby, to accept the offer, Mr Hornsby expressing the opinion that it was a very gracious act on the part of the Great Western Company to offer it.
Mr Boyd Carpenter stated that the engine would probably be taken out of traffic towards the end of this year or the beginning of 1931, but that the Committee would be advised later of the exact date.
Mr Rudgard produced a plan showing how he proposed to accommodate the engine in the Queen Street Museum and this was also approved by the Committee.

The Museum and the LNER having agreed in principle to accepting *City of Truro* from the GWR, Bywell then wrote to Boyd-Carpenter:

V. Boyd-Carpenter Esq.,
Yorkshire Farmers Union,
5 Bank Chambers,
Doncaster.   26th September 1930.
Dear Mr Boyd-Carpenter,
So as to keep things right I am sending you a draft of the minute regarding the offer of "The City of Truro" to the Railway Museum. Before I circulate the minute would you please say whether you agree that it correctly represents the facts. My delay in sending the draft is due to my having been in London for the past few days.
A duplicate copy of the draft minute is enclosed which you may like to show to Mr Collett. Maybe at a later stage of the proceedings when arrangements for the transit and reception of the engine require to be made, it will be advantage for the Great Western representatives to get into touch with our Company.
I will take care that it is not at any time lost sight of that you are responsible for the engine having been offered to the Museum and no doubt it will be possible to arrange for the last journey of "The City of Truro" to be made at a time when it will be convenient for you to be present.
Yours faithfully,
E.M. Bywell, Secretary & Curator of the Railway Museum.

The stage having thus been set, the LNER finally made its first formal contact with the GWR on the subject of *City of Truro* shortly before Christmas. The Museum probably wished to wait until the locomotive's withdrawal was more imminent.

C.B. Collett Esq.,   8th December 1930
Chief Mechanical Engineer,
Great Western Railway,
Swindon,
Wilts.
Dear Sir,

THE RAILWAY MUSEUM, YORK.
It has come to the knowledge of the Museum Committee through the medium of a railway enthusiast that the famous "City of Truro" engine is to be taken out of

traffic very shortly. As you will no doubt be aware the Railway Museum at York contains a number of engines of historic value, including the "Gladstone" which formerly ran on the London, Brighton & South Coast Railway and I am authorised by the Museum Committee to say that they would be pleased indeed if the "City of Truro" could also find a resting place there.

I obtained the dimensions of the "City of Truro" from one of your publications and the Engineer informs me that by a little re-arrangement of our exhibits there would just be space for its accommodation. I trust therefore to receive a favourable reply,
yours faithfully,
E.M. Bywell; Secretary & Curator of the Railway Museum.

The Museum Committee met again (its 23rd gathering) on February 2 1931, and Minute 167 recorded that LNER management had also asked the GWR to make City of Truro available to the Museum. Perhaps the GWR didn't wish to be seen to be getting over-excited about its past — certainly there was a rather surprising answer from the corridors of power at Paddington. The Minute read:

Arising out of Minute 163, the Secretary explained that to put the matter upon a more official basis Mr R. Bell, Assistant General Manager, had written to Mr Milne, General Manager of the Great Western Railway, suggesting that "The City of Truro" when withdrawn from traffic, might fittingly be preserved in the Museum. A reply from Mr Milne was read in which he stated that although he did not consider the engine to be of outstanding importance except that it was "true that it was the locomotive which attained the record speed of 102.3 miles per hour when hauling a special mail train from Plymouth to Bristol in May 1904," he would be prepared to ask his Directors to offer it.

The Committee, after reconsidering the question in the light of Mr Milne's letter, reaffirmed their desire to have the engine. It was thought that the addition of a Great Western engine, and particularly one that has held the world's speed record for so many years, would add materially to the interest of the Museum.

A fortnight later, the Great Western Railway nodded its assent to the Museum's request, in a letter from General Manager J. Milne:

Great Western Railway Company,
General Manager's Office,
Paddington Station, W2.
February 16th 1931.
G1/75837(63) PERSONAL
My dear Bell,
With reference to our previous correspondence regarding the "City of Truro": the matter was submitted to my Directors last week when they approved the proposal to present the engine to the Railway Museum at York on the understanding that if, at any time, this company wished the locomotive returned for any purpose, it would be entirely at our disposal.

I am requesting Mr Collett to proceed with the work of making the engine and tender presentable and will advise you further when they are ready for transit to York. It is proposed to forward them via Banbury and Doncaster and I assume that you will arrange free conveyance over your Company's system.

For your information, I may say that our Publicity Department are very anxious to issue a "story" to the press regarding the retirement of "City of Truro" and I should be grateful if you would see that no official announcement is made by your company or the Museum at the moment.
with kind regards,
yours sincerely,
J. Milne; General Manager, GWR.

Of interest in this letter is that the GWR publicity people certainly appreciated the locomotive's importance if Milne didn't (or purported not to!) and that the Board of Directors wished to retain an option to use the engine again at any stage, if they so wished! The LNER didn't waste any time, and Bell set pen to paper the following day:

XS749   PRIVATE 17th February 1931
J. Milne Esq.,
General Manager,
Great Western Railway,
Paddington Station, W2.
My dear Milne,
      "CITY OF TRURO" ENGINE.
G1/75837(63)
Thank you for your letter of February 16th. It is very good of your Directors to let the engine go to York and of course we will arrange to take the engine and tender forward from Banbury. We have asked our Locomotive Running Superintendent at York to arrange this direct with Mr Collett when the engine is ready to go.
We shall be happy to fall in with the wishes of your Publicity Department and have warned both the Museum Committee at York and our own Press Section here not to say a word on the subject until your Company have made their announcement.
with kind regards,
yours sincerely,
R. Bell.

Bell was as good as his word in making plans for getting City of Truro to York, and he was crystal clear in his orders that all lips should remain sealed:

The Chief General Manager,
LNER,
Kings Cross Station,
LONDON, N1.
Thos. Hornsby Esq.,
Divisional General Manager,
YORK,
XS 749   PERSONAL 17th February 1931.
My dear Hornsby,
      Great Western engine "City of Truro"
With further reference to your letter of January 8th, I now send you copy of a note from Mr Milne together with copy of my reply. Would you be kind enough to make arrangements on the lines indicated for getting the engine and tender to York and

instruct everybody to keep quiet about the addition to the Museum until the Great Western Company have spoken.
yours very truly,
R. Bell.

Following this correspondence the necessary arrangements were made, presumably the command of silence was obeyed, and about a month later this memo was circulated:

THE ENGINEER   20th March 1931
RAILWAY MUSEUM, YORK. ENGINE 'CITY OF TRURO'.
Referring to my letter of the 19th February: the Locomotive Running Superintendent informs me that Engine 'City of Truro' is leaving Swindon at 3.30 am today for York, via Banbury. It is travelling 'dead' by goods train.
Arrangements have been made for the engine to be put under cover on arrival at York until such time as it can be accommodated in the Museum.
Will you kindly let me know what arrangements you are making for placing it in the Museum and when you anticipate being able to locate it there.

Once the arrangements for 'City of Truro's' delivery to York were signed and sealed GWR General Manager J. Milne warmed to the idea even further, as indicated in a letter from R. Bell to LNER management at York:

The Chief General Manager,
LNER,
Kings Cross Station,
London, N1.

Divisional General Manager,
York.
XS49   16th April 1931
GREAT WESTERN ENGINE "CITY OF TRURO"
Mr Milne has written privately to the writer as follows:
"It has been suggested to me that a pamphlet might be prepared containing a detailed description of this engine and its historic run which could be placed on sale at the York Railway Museum. I do not know how the Museum authorities would regard this suggestion or whether it is the practice to have literature on sale, but perhaps you would be so good as to obtain their views on the matter. If they are favourable impressed with the idea, I should be pleased to arrange for a draft pamphlet to be prepared. At the same time, I should be grateful if you would kindly ascertain whether the Museum Committee are in possession of sufficient information to enable them to suitably label the engine; if not I shall be happy to supply any details required."
Would you be kind enough to ask your Museum Committee to consider the matter quickly and let me hear from you when you have found time to consider their views.
for R.L. Wedgwood,
R. Bell.

APPENDIX 4

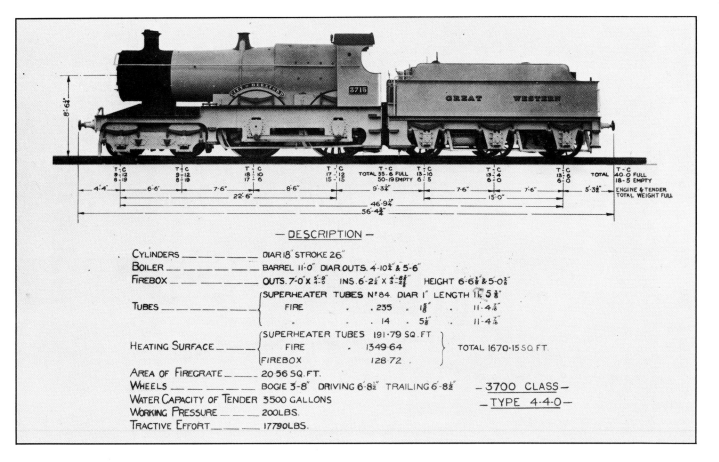

— DESCRIPTION —

CYLINDERS —— DIAR 18" STROKE 26"
BOILER —— BARREL 11'-0" DIAR OUTS. 4'-10¾" & 5'-6"
FIREBOX —— OUTS. 7'-0" X 5'-9"/4'-0" INS. 6'-2½" X 4'-8¾"/3'-2⅝" HEIGHT 6'-6⅜" & 5'-0⅜"
TUBES —— SUPERHEATER TUBES Nº 84. DIAR 1" LENGTH 11'-5⅜"; FIRE " . 235 " 1⅝" " 11'-4⁷⁄₁₆"; " " . 14 " 5⅛" " 11'-4⁷⁄₁₆"
HEATING SURFACE —— SUPERHEATER TUBES 191·79 SQ. FT; FIRE " 1349·64; FIREBOX 128·72 — TOTAL 1670·15 SQ. FT.
AREA OF FIREGRATE —— 20·56 SQ. FT.
WHEELS —— BOGIE 3'-8" DRIVING 6'-8½" TRAILING 6'-8½"
WATER CAPACITY OF TENDER 3500 GALLONS
WORKING PRESSURE —— 200 LBS.
TRACTIVE EFFORT —— 17790 LBS.

— 3700 CLASS —
— TYPE 4-4-0 —

ORIGINAL NUMBER	GWR RENUMBERING	NAME	BUILT OR REBUILT	WORKS NUMBER	SUPER HEATED	PISTON VALVES	WITH-DRAWN
3400	3700	*Durban**	R 4/07	1853	5/12	6/25	11/29
3401	3701	*Gibraltar**	R 2/07	1854	6/12	—	9/28
3402	3702	*Halifax**	R 12/08	1855	6/10	3/19	4/29
3403	3703	*Hobart**	R 2/09	1856	3/11	7/15	8/29
3404	3704	*Lyttelton*[1]*	R 10/07	1857	7/11	10/16	9/28
3405	3705	*Mauritius**	R 9/02	1858	6/11	2/18	9/28
3406	3706	*Melbourne**	R 1/08	1859	12/11	11/15	6/29
3407	3707	*Malta**	R 11/08	1860	10/10	4/20	4/29
3408	3708	*Ophir* (until* 9/07) then *Killarney*	R 5/07	1861	11/11	7/15	10/29
3409	3709	*Quebec**	R 11/07	1862	6/11	3/21	9/29
3433	3710	*City of Bath*	3/03	1993	9/11	11/18	9/28
3434	3711	*City of Birmingham*	5/03	1994	10/11	6/21	7/30
3435	3712	*City of Bristol*	5/03	1995	1/12	5/15	5/31
3436	3713	*City of Chester*	5/03	1996	9/10	4/17	12/29
3437	3714	*City of Gloucester*	5/03	1997	2/11	10/23[2]	11/29
3438	3715	*City of Hereford*	5/03	1998	6/11	3/18	10/29
3439	3716	*City of London*	5/03	1999	5/11	1/17	4/29
3440	3717	*City of Truro*	5/03	2000	9/11	11/15	3/31
3441	3718	*City of Winchester*	5/03	2001	6/11	—	10/27
3442	3719	*City of Exeter*	5/03	2002	10/11	5/16	4/29

[1]Spelled Lyttleton until 6/20.

[2]Date when first observed with piston valves, date of fitting not recorded.

*Locomotives rebuilt from 'Atbara' 4-4-0s.

APPENDIX 5

THIS appendix lists known allocations and stoppages at depots and workshops for the 'City' class as a whole from their entry into traffic as new locomotives, through to withdrawal. The list includes the allocations of Nos. 3400–3409 during their early years as 'Atbara' class 4-4-0s, prior to modification with the Standard No. 4 boilers as 'City' class locomotives.

This information was exhaustively researched by the late P.J.T. Reed from the archives of the British Transport Commission's Historical Records Department, Porchester Row, London, using the GWR's original Engine Record Cards. All BTC records are now maintained by the Public Record Office, Kew, London. Information reproduced courtesy of E.R. Mountford.

3400 (3700) *DURBAN*: PDN 10/01; SW 10/02; PDN 12/02; Salop 6/03; WW 1/04; Salop 7/04; WPN 10/05; SW 2/06; WPN 4/06; SW 3/07; WPN 5/07; SW 8/08; OXF 11/08; WPN 12/08; SW 1/10; OXF 4/10; SW 2/12; CDF 6/12; SW 12/13; WOS 5/14; OXF 10/17; SW 2/23; SW 5/23; SW 3/25; WPN 7/25; WW 3/27; WPN 10/27; TYS 7/29; LMTN 5/29; WPN 9/29; CONDEMNED 13/11/29.

3401 (3701) *GIBRALTAR*: Salop 9/01; WW 7/02; Salop 8/02; SW 8/03; Salop 11/03; SW 3/05; Salop 7/05; WW 2/06; Salop 3/06; SW 12/06; HFD 4/07; SW 11/09; HFD 2/10; SW 5/12; HFD 7/12; SW 9/12; HFD 11/12; SW 9/14; WOS 11/14; SW 6/16; WOS 9/16; SW 4/18; WPN 7/18; WW 9/22; WPN 10/22; SW 4/23; WPN 8/23; Salop 12/23; WPN 3/24; SW 5/25; WPN 8/25; WW 2/27; WPN 5/27; SW 7/28; CONDEMNED 30/9/28.

3402 (3702) *HALIFAX*: WEY 9/01; SW 3/02; WEY 4/02; S 11/02; SW 3/03; PDN 6/03; SW 10/04; CDF 1/05; SW 10/06; CDF 2/07; SW 10/08; CDF 2/09; SW 6/10; CDF 8/10; SW 12/11; BAN 5/12; OXF 7/12; SW 1/14; OXF 3/14; SW 3/16; OXF 7/16; WPN 10/18; SW 12/18; OXF 9/19; SW 11/22; OXF 1/23; PDNW 10/23; OXF 12/23; SW 10/24; OXF 1/27; SW 2/27; RDG 5/27; LMTN 8/28; CONDEMNED 11/4/29.

3403 (3703) *HOBART*: EXE 9/01; SW 2/02; EXE 4/02; SW 5/03; BL 8/03; SW 1/04; BL 3/04; SW 1/05; Salop 3/05; SW 10/06; WPN 1/07; SW 1/09; WPN 3/09; CHR 11/09; SW 1/10; WPN 3/10; SW 1/11; 5/11; Salop 8/11; WPN 2/12; SW 2/13; WPN 5/13; SW 5/15; WPN 9/15; SW 3/18; WW 7/18; CHR 8/18; WPN 12/19; SW 11/23; Salop 2/24; SW 6/24; BAN 9/24; SW 6/27; BAN 9/27; CONDEMNED 30/8/29.

3404 (3704) *LYTTLETON*: BL 9/01; SW 2/03; PDN 5/03; SW 10/04; CDF 1/05; SW 2/06; CDF 4/06; SW 9/07; CDF 11/07; FGD 1/08; LDR 7/08; SW 6/09; FGD 9/09; CARM 6/10; LDR 10/10; SW 6/11; CDF 9/11; SW 2/13; CDF 7/13; SW 6/15; WOS 9/15; SW 8/16; WOS 12/16; HFD 8/18; SW 12/19; BAN 20; SW 12/22; WPN 3/23; Salop 10/24; CHR 12/24; SW 3/25; WPN 5/25; WW 1/27; WPN 4/27; CHR 4/28; SW 8/28; CONDEMNED 11/9/28.

3405 (3705) *MAURITIUS*: CDF 9/01; SW 8/02; CDF 10/02; SW 10/03; CDF 12/03; SW 1/05; PDN 5/05; SW 10/06; PDN 1/07; SW 1/08; WPN 5/08; Salop 6/08; WPN 1/09; Salop 5/09; SW 11/09; WPN 2/10; CHR 12/10; WW 3/11; WPN 7/11; CHR 9/11; FGD 10/11; CHR 11/11; SW 9/12; WPN 12/12; SW 11/14; WOS 3/15; SW 10/17; WOS 3/18; SW 1/21; WOS 7/21; OXF 12/21; SW 10/23; RDG 1/24; SW 2/27; OXF 5/27; SW 6/28; CONDEMNED 21/9/28.

3406 (3706) *MELBOURNE*: WPN 11/01; Salop 1/02; SW 10/03; Salop 12/03; SW 2/06; Salop 6/06; SW 1/07; Salop 2/07; SW 11/07; WPN 2/08; CHR 6/08; SW 9/09; WPN 11/09; CHR 9/10; SW 12/10; W 2/11; CHR 6/11; SW 4/12; CHR 9/12; SW 7/13; CHR 10/13; SW 8/15; CHR 12/15; SW 6/17; SW 4/19; WPN 9/19; CREWE (Gresty Lane) 1/21; WPN 3/21; SW 9/22; WPN 10/22; SW 1/23; WPN 3/23; BAN 4/23; SW 10/24; BAN 1/25; SW 12/25; BAN 2/26; TYS 11/27; BAN 2/28; CONDEMNED 13/6/29.

3407 (3707) *MALTA*: CDF 10/01; SW 12/02; CDF 3/03; SW 2/04; NA 5/04; SW 10/05; NA 12/05; SW 11/06; NA 1/07; SW 9/08; NA 12/08; SW 10/10; NA 12/10; SW 11/11; WPN 4/12; SW 1/15; WPN 4/15; SW 4/17; WPN 7/17; SW 11/19; Salop /20; SW 2/23; BL 6/23 (WSM); SW 5/25; BL 8/25; TYS(W) 11/25; BL 1/26; SW 3/27; BL 10/27 (SPM-WSM-BL); CONDEMNED 11/4/29.

3408 (3708) *OPHIR* (until 9/07, renamed) *KILLARNEY*: CDF 12/01; SW 2/03; CDF 5/03; SW 10/04; PDN 12/04; SW 1/05; CDF 3/05; SW 9/05; CDF 11/05; SW 4/07; CDF 7/07; SW 11/08; CDF 12/08; SW 1/10; CDF 3/10; SW 9/11; BL 11/11; SW 9/13; BL 11/13; SW 4/15; BL 7/15; SW 7/18; BL 11/18; SW /20; WOS 2/21; SW 6/23; WOS 10/23; SW 3/25; WPN 6/25; Salop 7/25; WW 11/26; Salop 1/27; WW 4/27; Salop 7/27; SW 5/28; Salop 9/28; SW 10/29; CONDEMNED 30/10/29.

3409 (3709) *QUEBEC*: PDN 10/01; SW 4/03; PDN 7/03; SW 10/04; PDN 1/05; SW 3/06; PDN 5/06; SW 7/07; PDN 1/08; SW 5/09; PDN 10/09; SW 5/11; CDF 7/11; SW 7/13; EXE 7/13; SW 2/15; RDG 5/15; SW 1/17; RDG 5/17; PDN 6/18; W11/18; RDN 3/19; SW /20; CHR 4/21; SW 5/23; OXF 9/23; SW 4/26; OXF 9/26; SW 8/27; CONDEMNED 6/9/29.

3433 (3710) *CITY OF BATH*: PDN 4/03; BL 4/04; PDN 6/04; SW 10/04; PDN 1/05; SW 3/06; PDN 6/06; SW 7/07; PDN 10/07; SW 3/09; PDN 7/09; SW 10/09; PDN 11/09; SW 8/11; PDN 11/11; SW 4/14; WOS 9/14; SW 8/16; WPN 10/16; SW 8/18; WPN 12/18; CHR 1/19; SW 4/21; TN 9/21; SW 11/23; WPN 1/24; CHR 3/25; SW 6/25; WPN 9/25; WW 12/26; WPN 4/27; WW 9/27; WPN 12/27; CHR 8/28; CONDEMNED 21/9/28.

3434 (3711) *CITY OF BIRMINGHAM*: PDN 6/03; SW 4/04; LA 7/04 (PLY); SW 7/05; WPN 10/05; Salop 3/06; WW 10/06; Salop 12/06; SW 5/07; WPN 9/07; SW 1/09; WPN 7/09; SW 10/10; WPN 12/10; Salop 7/11; SW 2/12; WPN 7/12; SW 10/13; CDF 1/14; SW 4/16; CHR 7/16; TYS W 3/17; CHR 8/17; SW 8/18; WPN 1/19; CHR 3/19; CHR 3/19; SW 3/21; CHR 7/21; SW 7/22; CHR 11/22; WW 7/23; WPN 11/23; SW 5/25; WPN 8/25; LMTN 2/27; SW 2/28; WPN 4/28; CHR 8/28; WPN 4/29; TYS W 5/29; WPN 7/29; LMTN 5/30; CONDEMNED 28/7/30.

3435 (3712) *CITY OF BRISTOL*: BL 4/03; SW 9/04; BL 12/04; SW 1/05; BL 3/05; SW 6/06; BL 10/06; SW 7/08; BL 9/08; SW 1/10; BL 3/10; SW 9/10; BL 10/10; SW 11/11; BL 4/12; SW 9/12; BL 12/12; SW 11/13; BL 3/14; SW 3/15; BL 6/15; SW 4/18; BL 10/18; SW 5/23; CHR 9/23; SW 4/18; BL 10/18; SW 5/23; CHR 9/23; SW 4/18; BL 10/18; SW 5/23; CHR 6/25; SW 8/27; PDN 11/27; RDG 12/27 (BASINGTOKE); RDG 6/30; CONDEMNED 23/5/31.

3436 (3713) *CITY OF CHESTER*: PDN 4/03; SW 3/04; EXE 6/04 (NA); BL 7/05; SW 3/06; BL 5/06; SW 6/07; PDN 9/07; SW 6/09; WPN 10/09; SW 10/10; WPN 12/10; CHR 9/11; SW 2/12; WPN 7/12; SW 8/14; WPN 11/14; CHR 3/16; SW 10/16; CHR 1/17; SW 5/19; WPN 11/19; BAN 9/22; WPN 11/22; SW 4/23; CHR 7/23; SW 3/23; CHR 7/23; SW 3/25; CHR 5/25; WW 12/25; CHR 2/26; WW 3/26; CHR 7/26; SW 5/27; CHR 9/27; WW 12/28; CHR 9/29; WPN 11/29; CONDEMNED 6/12/29.

3437 (3714) *CITY OF GLOUCESTER*: EXE 4/03; SW 8/04; NA 11/04; BL 6/05; SW 3/06; BL 5/06; WPN 2/07; BL 5/07; SW 2/08; BL 6/08; SW 6/09; BL 10/09; SW 1/11; BL 3/11; SW 10/12; LDR 2/13; SW 10/14; WOS 1/15; SW 12/15; WOS 1/16; SW 5/17; WOS 10/17; SW 4/21; WOS 5/21; OXF 12/21; LMTN 4/23; OXF 6/23; SW 7/23; OXF 11/23; SW 5/26; OXF 9/26; PDNW 2/27; OXF 5/27; CONDEMNED 23/11/29.

3438 (3715) *CITY OF HEREFORD*: PDN 5/03; SW 7/04; PDN 9/04; SW 12/04; PDN 2/05; SW 6/06; PDN 9/06; PDN 9/07; SW 10/07; PDN 12/07; W 3/08; PDN 5/08; SW 5/09; PDN 9/09; SW 5/11; PDN 6/11; SW 10/12; BL 3/13; SW 7/15; PDN 12/15; RDG 1/17; SW 11/17; RDG 4/18; SW /20; RDG 1/21; PDN 3/22; OXF 8/22; SW 5/24; OXF 7/26; SW 3/27; CHR 6/27; WW 7/28; CHR 10/28; Salop 5/29; CHR 6/29; CONDEMNED 21/10/29.

3439 (3716) *CITY OF LONDON*: PDN 5/03; SW 2/04; PDN 6/04; SW 2/05; PDN 5/05; SW 6/06; PDN 9/06; SW 10/07; PDN 12/07; SW 3/09; PDN 7/09; SW 4/11; PDN 6/11; SW 10/12; PDN 2/13; RDG 10/14; SW 6/15; BL 10/15; SW 12/16; BL 2/17; TN 7/17; SW 1/18; BL 5/18; TN 9/18; BL 12/19; SW 6/21; S 10/21 (WES 12/21); S 1/22; SW 9/24; S 12/24; BL 4/26; SW 10/26; BL 2/27 (WSM); CONDEMNED 11/4/29.

3440 (3717) *CITY OF TRURO*: EXE 6/03; SW 12/05; NA 3/06; SW 8/07; NA 10/07; SW 12/08; NA 3/09; EXE 7/10; NAW 9/11; EXE 12/10; SW 9/11; NA 11/11; SW 7/13; BL 11/13; TYS W 3/15; BL 4/15; SW 6/15; BL 11/15; SW 8/16; BL 9/16; SW 11/19; TN 7/20; SW 10/21; BL (WSM) 3/22; SW 5/23; WPN 7/23; BL 8/23; BAN 10/23; BAN 10/23; SW 8/25; WPN 10/25; Salop 3/26; SW 11/27; Salop 6/28; SW 11/29; Salop 11/29; CONDEMNED 12/3/31 AND PRESENTED TO THE RAILWAY MUSEUM, YORK.

3441 (3718) *CITY OF WINCHESTER*: PDN 5/03; SW 7/04; PDN 9/04; SW 1/06; PDN 3/06; SW 6/07; PDN 9/07; SW 9/08; NA 12/08; SW 4/10; NA 6/10; SW 5/11; PDN 7/11; SW 2/13; BL 4/13; SW 12/13; BL 3/14; SW 11/15; BL 3/16; SW 3/18; WOS 7/18; SW 6/21; RDG 11/21; PDN 3/24; SW 6/24; PDN 7/24; CONDEMNED 4/10/27.

3442 (3719) *CITY OF EXETER*: EXE 6/03; SW 6/04; EXE 8/04; PLY 12/04; BL 6/05; SW 2/06; BL 6/06; SW 3/07; EXE 6/07; NA 12/07; NA 12/07; SW 2/10; BL 5/10; SW 9/11; BL 12/11; SW 2/12; BL 4/12; CDF 2/13; WPN 4/13; BL 5/13; SW 12/13; WOS 5/14; SW 3/16; WOS 7/10; SW 4/18; WPN 10/18; CHR 5/19; WPN 7/19; SW /20; CHR 2/21; WW 9/21; CHR 4/22; SW 3/23; CHR 5/23; WPN 7/24; TYS W 4/25; WPN 7/25; SW 12/26; OXF 3/27; CONDEMNED 11/4/29.

KEY:
BAN — Banbury; BL — Bristol Bath Road; CARM — Carmarthen; CDF — Cardiff; CHR — Chester; EXE — Exeter; FGD — Fishguard; HFD — Hereford; LA (PLY) Plymouth Laira; LDR — Llandore; LMTN — Leamington; NA — Newton Abbot; OXF — Oxford; PDN — Westbourne Park until 1906, then Old Oak Common; RDG — Reading; Salop — Shrewsbury; SPM — St Phillips Marsh, Bristol; S — Swindon; SW — Swindon Works; WES — Westbury; WSM — Weston Super Mare; WPN — Wolverhampton; WW — Wolverhampton Works; WOS — Worcester.